Responsive Mobile Design

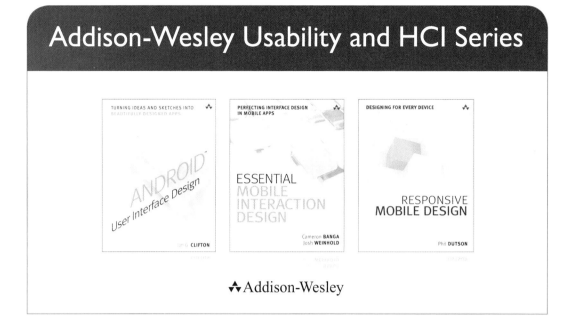

Praise for
Responsive Mobile Design

"Whether you're building or refining your skill set, *Responsive Mobile Design* is the quintessential guide to getting up to speed with modern web practices. Phil's unique background and expertise grant him insights that both the hardcore programmer and pixel perfect designer will find invaluable."

—**Jacob R. Stuart**, Web/UI Designer

"It's impossible to build for the web today without taking various screen sizes and form factors into account; you never know if your user will be on a phone, tablet, or desktop. This book helps lay the groundwork for building responsive web designs. It's really a must-read."

—**Cameron Banga**, Co-founder, 9magnets, LLC

"Anyone looking for a comprehensive book on responsive design tactics would do well to pick up a copy of *Responsive Mobile Design*. Phil does a stellar job of breaking down the how and why of RWD in this practical guide to designing for a wide spectrum of screen sizes and devices."

—**Dennis Kardys**, Design Director, WSOL

"While the three initial technical ingredients of RWD (fluid grids, flexible images, and media queries) still stand true, building a site today requires much more thought and know-how than it used to. This book will take you beyond the basics and teach you the ins and outs of modern web development."

—**Erik Runyon**, Director of Web Communications, University of Notre Dame

"Phil Dutson unveils a dummy-proof treasure trove of essential mobile design advice, resources, and examples bound to enlighten designers and developers alike. This book belongs on every web designer's shelf—a comprehensive guide to return to time and time again."

—**Kaylee White**, Web Designer, SEO.com

Responsive Mobile Design

Designing for Every Device

Phil Dutson

✦✦ Addison-Wesley

Upper Saddle River, NJ • Boston • Indianapolis • San Francisco
New York • Toronto • Montreal • London • Munich • Paris • Madrid
Capetown • Sydney • Tokyo • Singapore • Mexico City

For information about buying this title in bulk quantities, or for special sales opportunities (which may include electronic versions; custom cover designs; and content particular to your business, training goals, marketing focus, or branding interests), please contact our corporate sales department at corpsales@pearsoned.com or (800) 382-3419.

For government sales inquiries, please contact governmentsales@pearsoned.com.

For questions about sales outside the U.S., please contact international@pearsoned.com.

Visit us on the Web: informit.com/aw

Library of Congress Control Number: 2014944246

ISBN-13: 978-0-133-88821-8

ISBN-10: 0-133-88821-5

Text printed in the United States on recycled paper at R.R. Donnelley in Crawfordsville, Indiana.

First printing: September 2014

Editor-in-Chief
Mark Taub

Executive Editor
Laura Lewin

Development Editor
Sheri Cain

Managing Editor
Kristy Hart

Senior Project Editor
Lori Lyons

Copy Editor
Krista Hansing Editorial Services

Indexer
Tim Wright

Proofreader
Debbie Williams

Technical Reviewers
Cameron Banga
Dennis Kardys
Jacob Stuart

Editorial Assistant
Olivia Basegio

Cover Designer
Chuti Prasertsith

Compositor
Nonie Ratcliff

Manufacturing Buyer
Dan Uhrig

To my friends and family, who remind me to look at everything through the eyes of an inquisitive 5-year-old without fear of mashing buttons until everything is working properly.

—Phil

Contents-at-a-Glance

Contents

PREFACE

The phrase "Responsive Mobile Design" doesn't really roll off the tongue, and even when placed under a microscope it tends to shift and blur, making it difficult to gain a full appreciation for what it is.

When you boil it down, it comes down to a paradigm shift. In breadth of design, this isn't really a new concept. It is more like the time when you first realized you could draw things in a third-dimensional perspective, and suddenly a new fascination with cubes, spheres, focal-points, and shadows started to overtake most of your sketches.

Being able to step back and realize that people want information as soon as possible, and having it fit on the device they happen to have at the moment, you can gain an appreciation for making sure that they get what they want in the most aesthetically pleasing way possible.

That is Responsive Mobile Design: the fusing of content, structure, and beauty to deliver experiences that users will continue to keep coming back to.

This book is full of my experiences with mobile devices, design, and even a smidgen of code that can help get your creation into the hands of millions of mobile users in the best way possible. Along the way, some topics will be lightly brushed over while others will have their intricacies beat upon like the soothing double-bass of your favorite Swedish-metal band.

To effectively use this book, you should have some experience with web design or development. That being said, this should also make an excellent resource for project and team managers who would like to learn current methodology and concepts they can use with their team.

Some topics are just not easily covered, or covered in proper detail, without an accompanying site with which to follow along or see some examples. I have created a website that you can leverage for various tools, tips, tutorials, and examples. Visit www.mobiledesignrecipes.com/ on your desktop or mobile device to find these resources.

You can also reach out to me on Google+ (+PhilDutson) or Twitter (@dutsonpa).

ABOUT THE AUTHOR

Phil Dutson is a Solution Architect over client-side and mobile implementation for ICON Health & Fitness. He is the author of *Sams Teach Yourself jQuery Mobile in 24 Hours*; *jQuery, jQuery UI, and jQuery Mobile Recipes and Examples*; and *The Android Developer's Cookbook, 2nd Edition*. He enjoys learning and writing about technology, and spreading enlightenment to the world one portal at a time with his sons playing Ingress.

ACKNOWLEDGMENTS

Creating a book is a monumental feat, but there are major players who help the process finish in a timely manner. First, I want to thank Laura Lewin for all her work and the dedication she put into this project. I would also like to thank Olivia Basegio for all of the last-minute emails and replies to random questions that I seem to send her. This book could not have happened without the dedication of the production team including Kristy Hart, Lori Lyons, Krista Hansing, Mark Taub, and all the other unsung heroes who make books like this polish into diamonds.

I have a special thank you for the extremely talented, remarkable, and absolutely brilliant resources who are Cameron Banga, Dennis Kardys, and Jacob Stuart. I appreciate the work that each of you put into being my technical editors. Thank you for all the insight, help, and comments you contributed to the flow, understanding, and clarity of each chapter. Thanks also to Sheri Cain, who as my development editor, put the reins on the project to make sure that my tangents made sense and that each chapter had clarity and focus from beginning to end.

I also want to thank my family for allowing me to disappear so many nights a week and still think I'm a pretty cool guy. Without the help of Ethan, Kile, Josie, Sam, and Anna, I wouldn't have anyone to use for the images that added a personal touch to the sample designs and tutorials in this book.

PART I

CREATING A RESPONSIVE LAYOUT

CHAPTER 1

CONTENT MATTERS

The most important step in creating a responsive site is often the most overlooked. Many designers like to begin work with mood-boards, wireframes, or even in-browser working prototypes. All these are useful in the design process and definitely should have a place in your workflow. However, you need to start asking yourself immediately what the real purpose behind your design is.

The message, both copy and visuals, is what makes up the content of your site. Content is crucial to delivering a site that not only performs, but also converts well.

Whether you are creating a site that is selling a service, a product, or an enterprise eCommerce solution, the content you deliver will be the driving force that motivates users to sign up, use, recommend, and encourage their friends to use that service, product, or solution.

This chapter discusses the various facets of content creation and delivery.

What Makes Up Content

In recent years, content has been a consideration, but it has never seemed to have earned the front seat in design. Designers and developers used to be able to rely on site age, in-bound links, and all the right keywords used in all the right places. These tactics guaranteed a site a rise to the very top of the search results, and users came in droves to visit the site.

Times have changed. You now need to focus on the actual content of your site. Search engines are now interested in the *value* and *quality* of your site content, both of which are measured in several ways:

- Social traffic, sharing, and posting from popular services such as Facebook, Twitter, and Google+
- Site copy that is relevant to the product or service
- Outbound links that are relevant to the page or product of the current page
- Minimized link and keyword stuffing
- Spelling, grammar, and presentation of your content
- Images, videos, and expanded copy added where appropriate
- Original or inspired content that does not duplicate other work

Knowing this, let's look at several factors that go into content creation.

Gathering Information

Getting started on information gathering can be as simple as sitting around a table with a group of colleagues or coworkers and discussing thoughts on your site, service, or product. Although it can feel similar to a brainstorming session, this really is more like an opportunity to do some "opinion farming." As you discuss your project, take notes on not only what your colleagues say, but how they say it. To help you gather opinions, you need to break down any silos your company has for this meeting. Bring in members from different teams and let them know their opinion counts. Agreement isn't the issue here; all thoughts should be shared. Grab another designer, add one or two developers, and also bring in a member of the user experience (UX) team, a project manager (for the 10,000-foot-view), and someone from the marketing team. Take note of the phrasing as well as the emotions shared as these experts express their thoughts and opinions; you can draw on these emotions later in the copy, typography, images, art direction, and even the colors you decide to use. If you find yourself lacking coworkers or colleagues, you still have other resources for information gathering. Visiting popular review sites or even large eCommerce sites with product reviews can provide inspiration and opinions.

On some sites, such as Amazon, many products have been "review hijacked" and are perfect targets for content gathering. In these reviews, you can find the very best in satire, original content, humor, and every emotion in between. (For a prime example of an excellent review hijack, check out the "Three Moon Wolf" T-shirt on Amazon, at www.amazon.com/ The-Mountain-Three-Short-Sleeve/dp/B002HJ377A.) In terms of content, these reviews give the product, as well as the Amazon site in this case, valuable content as links to the page are repeatedly shared over social media and other sites. As an added bonus, new reviews are put on display daily, which keeps new content churning and increases the value of the page to search engines, thus improving the effectiveness of their search engine optimization (SEO). In terms of content gathering, you can look for opinions and writing styles that appeal to you and others. Some reviews even discuss alternate methods of use for the product. This is a fantastic way to crowd-source your product, to at least give you an opportunity to correct public perception of what the product or project is good for.

Remember that content should also be engaging. No one likes to read page and after page of dry, technical drivel in 12-point sans-serif font. People crave variety, choice, and anything that stands out. Comparing visual media with print or digital media might seem like a stretch, but using commercials is a great way to find out what works—and what does not. My personal favorite time of year for commercials is generally around January and February. This is because all of the Super Bowl commercials start to air, and I get a great sense of what works and what goes too far. Whether it is zany, comical, or just across the line of what is socially acceptable, these commercials demonstrate the power of content in 30 to 60 seconds. Within a day or two after the commercials have aired, you get a great gauge on which commercials hit the spot and which ones completely missed the mark. You can then deconstruct this information into what might work for your project.

Another piece of information gathering not to ignore is talking to the people who create your product. If you are working with hard goods, you should be talking to the manufacturers, engineers, industrial designers, and testers to get their feedback on the process of creating the product. Sometimes these people see what could potentially be fatal flaws with your product, but they do not pass along their concerns simply because they are not asked to share their opinion. If you are working with a digital good or service, you should be chatting with software engineers, developers, admins, and content managers to get feedback on the difficulty of implementation, the availability of third-party integration, and whether they would ever use the service for themselves. Getting technical feedback is crucial because it helps you decide later what needs to be shared with consumers and also make you the authority on the content you will be presenting on your site.

After gathering ideas, opinions, emotions, and technical details from people, media, and reviews or similar crowd-sourced pools, you are ready to start distilling the information to define the message you will share as part of your content.

Defining the Message

Gathering information can be an exciting distraction, but at some point, you need to sit down and start evaluating what you have gathered and how it properly applies to your project.

To help you define the message you will use as part of your content, ask yourself the following questions about the product you are trying to show the user while analyzing the information you gathered:

- How does the product make me feel?
- What will the product do for me?
- Will people be excited about the product and share it with their friends?
- How does knowing the technical aspects of the product help me sell or deliver it?

As you work through the list, you should get a feel for what your product is and what makes it unique. Your gathered information of opinions, feedback, and reviews or testimonials will help you map out the best features and benefits.

From here, you can further distill the information to major key points or features. To help visualize the data, gather common words, elements, or themes and graph them. The pie graph in Figure 1.1 shows some common phrases from a sample project.

Figure 1.2 shows a radar graph that helps you focus on where to spend time refining the focus of the content.

Remember that your content should be concise and clear, and should give potential users a reason why they need your product. Let's look at why choosing the right content is so important.

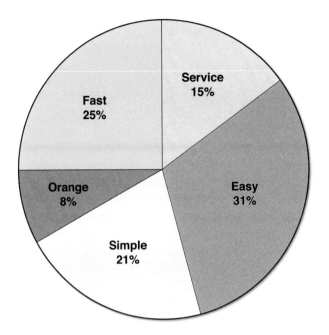

Figure 1.1 A pie chart that shows the amount of data per keyword or term.

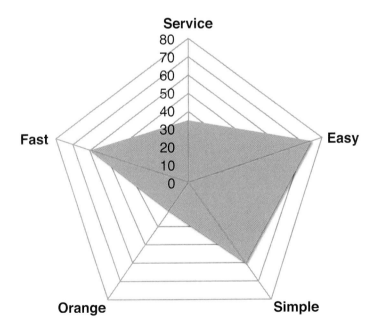

Figure 1.2 A radar chart showing the frequency of relevant terms and data.

Choosing the Right Content

From site performance to SEO, choosing the right content creates either a site that users frequent or one they go out of their way to avoid.

When given a design specification, designers sometimes have difficulty separating creative vision from what actually needs to be done. This isn't necessarily bad. In fact, I am a firm believer that every good design contains a piece of the designer who created it. Unfortunately, problems can arise when a specification lacks proper consideration and emphasis regarding the content that should be included in the design. Unnecessary complexity results and can detract from important considerations such as content performance, SEO, and user expectation. It can almost feel like someone telling you to design a bike but then not telling you what type, who will ride it, and any limitations or conditions it needs to perform against. In real-world design terms, considerations such as how your design will perform on a mobile device and how users are going to find your site help you get started without having to go back and reduce or scrap your entire design.

Content Performance

For every image, font, icon, sprite, framework, and plugin that you want to use in your design, you increase the number of requests and resources that you must send to the user. Let's break this down by looking at a simple static site that contains the following:

- index.html
- styles.css
- scripts.js
- framework.js
- hero.jpg
- sprites.svg

As you can see, the site includes six files. When a user loads the page for the first time, six HTTP requests are made to download and store assets. Depending on the connection type, the connection speed, and the size of the assets served, the page could take anywhere from 1 second to upward of 15 seconds. The fewer assets you serve, the fewer requests the user's browser must make and the faster the page is rendered and displayed to the user. Figure 1.3 shows a waterfall chart of a browser making requests to a server for a simple site.

URL	Status	Domain	Size	Remote IP	Timeline	
▶ GET dutsonpa.com	200 OK	dutsonpa.com	7.9 KB	199.83.132.254 80		435ms
▶ GET reset.css	200 OK	dutsonpa.com	888 B	199.83.132.254 80		200ms
▶ GET style.css	200 OK	dutsonpa.com	1.5 KB	199.83.132.254 80		200ms
▶ GET small.css	200 OK	dutsonpa.com	330 B	199.83.132.254 80		200ms
▶ GET zepto.js	200 OK	dutsonpa.com	8.4 KB	199.83.132.254 80		201ms
▶ GET main.js	200 OK	dutsonpa.com	361 B	199.83.132.254 80		199ms
▶ GET categories.png	200 OK	dutsonpa.com	144 B	199.83.132.254 80		279ms
7 requests			19.5 KB			919ms (onload: 926ms)

Figure 1.3   A waterfall chart loading a small site.

Complex sites tend to serve many more files, and eCommerce sites serve even more. Figure 1.4 shows the waterfall chart from a larger eCommerce site. Note that the site uses so many different images that they cannot be easily combined into a sprite; they add many requests to the site load. Tracking pixels, affiliate pixels, included JavaScript, and multiple CSS files are also not combined and add delay to the page when rendered by the browser when a user initially visits the site.

> ### Tip
>
> Adding third-party content can help you analyze your site traffic and campaign effectiveness, but it can have serious side effects on the user experience. Many of these pixels, widgets, and solutions are hosted from servers that might not be near you. Even worse, they can leave your users with an unresponsive page that does nothing until all items have been loaded. Carefully choose the third-party content you include on your site.

After reviewing Figures 1.3 and 1.4, you can see that not only do many requests occur, but the amount of time to load the page increases dramatically. Many developers are passionate about this issue of web development when they talk about site bloat, content blocking, and sluggish rendering times.

> ### Tip
>
> You might have heard the terms *lazy load, deferred loading,* or *asynchronous delivery.* All relate to the same concept. When a web browser loads a page, it runs through a specific order to download files, assemble them, and display them onscreen. JavaScript files, which make up a considerable portion of third-party content, including tracking pixels and widgets, block other site assets from loading. This can be solved by using a lazy-loading, deferred, or asynchronous technique that allows the rest of the site (styles, images, and text) to load before the scripts run. Users can thus continue to use the site with features loading on the page when ready instead of having to wait for those features.

URL	Status	Domain	Size	Remote IP	Timeline
GET Treadmills	200 OK	proform.com	15.8 KB	63.225.63.68:80	1.52s
GET bootstrap.min	200 OK	proform.com	17.9 KB	63.225.63.68:80	119ms
GET easy-respons	200 OK	proform.com	918 B	63.225.63.68:80	66ms
GET style.css	200 OK	proform.com	19.1 KB	63.225.63.68:80	135ms
GET jquery.min.js	200 OK	proform.com	32.0 KB	63.225.63.68:80	87ms
GET include.js?dor	200 OK	whoson.iconfitness.com	1.3 KB	63.225.63.224:80	148ms
GET respond.src.js	200 OK	proform.com	3.6 KB	63.225.63.68:80	150ms
GET header_call_ic	304 Not Modified	images.iconcdn.com	0 B	68.142.123.254:80	264ms
GET mo_logo1.png	304 Not Modified	images.iconcdn.com	0 B	68.142.123.254:80	251ms
GET mo_cart1.png	304 Not Modified	images.iconcdn.com	0 B	68.142.123.254:80	262ms
GET mo_info1.png	304 Not Modified	images.iconcdn.com	0 B	68.142.123.254:80	245ms
GET mo_bars.png	304 Not Modified	images.iconcdn.com	0 B	68.142.123.254:80	267ms
GET dojo.js	200 OK	proform.com	119.9 KB	63.225.63.68:80	374ms
GET tracking.js	200 OK	proform.com	894 B	63.225.63.68:80	135ms
GET TealeafSDKCo	200 OK	proform.com	20.8 KB	63.225.63.68:80	256ms
GET TealeafSDK.js	200 OK	proform.com	20 B	63.225.63.68:80	116ms
GET s_code_http.js	200 OK	proform.com	21.1 KB	63.225.63.68:80	278ms
GET mo_phone1.p	304 Not Modified	images.iconcdn.com	0 B	68.142.123.254:80	147ms
GET header_bml.p	304 Not Modified	images.iconcdn.com	0 B	68.142.123.254:80	119ms
GET 1x1.gif	200 OK	img.iconcdn.com	35 B	63.225.63.180:443	14ms
GET 1x1.gif	304 Not Modified	images.iconcdn.com	0 B	68.142.123.254:80	113ms
GET interest_icon.	Aborted	img.iconcdn.com	0 B	63.225.63.180:80	4.01s
GET bml_logo_sml	Aborted	img.iconcdn.com	0 B	63.225.63.180:80	4.01s
GET shipping_icon	Aborted	img.iconcdn.com	0 B	63.225.63.180:80	4.01s
GET ift_icon.png	Aborted	img.iconcdn.com	0 B	63.225.63.180:80	4.01s
GET header_bg.jp	304 Not Modified	images.iconcdn.com	0 B	68.142.123.254:80	111ms
GET logos_sprite_	304 Not Modified	images.iconcdn.com	0 B	68.142.123.254:80	111ms
GET nav_dark_gra	304 Not Modified	images.iconcdn.com	0 B	68.142.123.254:80	111ms
GET nav_cap_left.	304 Not Modified	images.iconcdn.com	0 B	68.142.123.254:80	173ms
GET nav_cap_right	304 Not Modified	images.iconcdn.com	0 B	68.142.123.254:80	172ms
GET nav_light_gra	304 Not Modified	images.iconcdn.com	0 B	68.142.123.254:80	170ms
GET nav_transition	304 Not Modified	images.iconcdn.com	0 B	68.142.123.254:80	185ms
GET sprite_sheet_	304 Not Modified	images.iconcdn.com	0 B	68.142.123.254:80	202ms
GET sale_banner_1	304 Not Modified	images.iconcdn.com	0 B	68.142.123.254:80	206ms
GET bg1340_top.j	304 Not Modified	images.iconcdn.com	0 B	68.142.123.254:80	228ms
GET stars_sprite.p	304 Not Modified	images.iconcdn.com	0 B	68.142.123.254:80	227ms
GET buttons_sprit	304 Not Modified	images.iconcdn.com	0 B	68.142.123.254:80	217ms
GET header_top.pr	304 Not Modified	images.iconcdn.com	0 B	68.142.123.254:80	242ms
GET bg1340_botto	304 Not Modified	images.iconcdn.com	0 B	68.142.123.254:80	312ms
GET blue_header.p	304 Not Modified	images.iconcdn.com	0 B	68.142.123.254:80	258ms
GET dojo_en-us.js	200 OK	proform.com	1.7 KB	63.225.63.68:80	8.1ms
GET s3234763064	Aborted	metrics.iconfitness.com	0 B	66.235.139.176:80	8.01s
GET bootstrap.js	304 Not Modified	c.compete.com	0 B	96.17.228.16:80	29ms
GET gtm.js?id=GT	200 OK	googletagmanager.com	11.7 KB	74.125.239.126:80	118ms
GET ga.js	304 Not Modified	google-analytics.com	0 B	74.125.239.130:80	55ms
GET stat.gif?u=75.	200 OK	whoson.iconfitness.com	43 B	63.225.63.224:80	29ms
GET invite.js?dom:	200 OK	whoson.iconfitness.com	2.3 KB	63.225.63.224:80	40ms
GET AjaxShopCoun	200 OK	proform.com	98 B	63.225.63.68:80	25ms
GET functions.js	200 OK	proform.com	1.2 KB	63.225.63.68:80	26ms
GET fodal-11.041-	200 OK	proform.com	2.0 KB	63.225.63.68:80	25ms
GET jRespond.min	200 OK	proform.com	765 B	63.225.63.68:80	29ms
GET forms.js	200 OK	proform.com	1.7 KB	63.225.63.68:80	31ms
GET addtocart.js	200 OK	proform.com	330 B	63.225.63.68:80	40ms
GET jquery.pixity.r	200 OK	proform.com	623 B	63.225.63.68:80	47ms
GET ServicesEvent	200 OK	proform.com	844 B	63.225.63.68:80	48ms
GET jquery.lazyloa	200 OK	proform.com	1.1 KB	63.225.63.68:80	70ms
GET blank.gif	200 OK	proform.com	43 B	63.225.63.68:80	127ms
GET __utm.gif?utm	200 OK	google-analytics.com	35 B	74.125.239.130:80	56ms
GET __utm.gif?utm	200 OK	google-analytics.com	35 B	74.125.239.131:80	48ms
GET conversion.js	304 Not Modified	googleadservices.com	0 B	74.125.239.109:80	51ms
GET PFTL99912_zi	Aborted	img.iconcdn.com	0 B	63.225.63.180:80	8.01s
GET CommonCont	200 OK	proform.com	2.1 KB	63.225.63.68:80	37ms
GET common.js	200 OK	proform.com	464 B	63.225.63.68:80	31ms
GET CommonCont	200 OK	proform.com	5.3 KB	63.225.63.68:80	42ms
GET MessageHelpe	200 OK	proform.com	4.5 KB	63.225.63.68:80	27ms
GET StoreCommor	200 OK	proform.com	11.1 KB	63.225.63.68:80	49ms
GET ServicesDecla	200 OK	proform.com	5.5 KB	63.225.63.68:80	28ms
GET CategoryDisp	200 OK	proform.com	19.6 KB	63.225.63.68:80	81ms
GET ItemFileWrite!	200 OK	proform.com	7.8 KB	63.225.63.68:80	39ms
GET ItemFileReadS	200 OK	proform.com	8.7 KB	63.225.63.68:80	37ms
GET filter.js	200 OK	proform.com	1020 B	63.225.63.68:80	27ms
GET simpleFetch.js	200 OK	proform.com	1.5 KB	63.225.63.68:80	36ms
GET sorter.js	200 OK	proform.com	1.5 KB	63.225.63.68:80	21ms
GET PFTL99513_s	304 Not Modified	images.iconcdn.com	0 B	68.142.123.254:80	51ms
GET PFTL99912_s	304 Not Modified	images.iconcdn.com	0 B	68.142.123.254:80	46ms
GET PFTL11012_s	200 OK	images.iconcdn.com	10.5 KB	68.142.123.254:80	331ms
GET PFTL11011_s	304 Not Modified	images.iconcdn.com	0 B	68.142.123.254:80	44ms
GET PFTL13011_s	304 Not Modified	images.iconcdn.com	0 B	68.142.123.254:80	87ms
GET PFTL14611_s	304 Not Modified	images.iconcdn.com	0 B	68.142.123.254:80	58ms
GET PFTL17112_s	304 Not Modified	images.iconcdn.com	0 B	68.142.123.254:80	155ms
GET PFTL20012_s	304 Not Modified	images.iconcdn.com	0 B	68.142.123.254:80	115ms
GET PFTL40012_s	200 OK	images.iconcdn.com	10.6 KB	68.142.123.254:80	321ms
GET PFTL30012_s	200 OK	images.iconcdn.com	12.0 KB	68.142.123.254:80	359ms
GET PFTL59513_s	200 OK	images.iconcdn.com	6.2 KB	68.142.123.254:80	347ms
GET PFTL14511_s	304 Not Modified	images.iconcdn.com	0 B	68.142.123.254:80	69ms
GET PFTL79513_s	304 Not Modified	images.iconcdn.com	0 B	68.142.123.254:80	45ms
GET poll.gif?d=ww	200 OK	whoson.iconfitness.com	43 B	63.225.63.224:80	117ms
87 requests			386.4 KB		10.55s (onload: 10.44s)

Figure 1.4   Waterfall chart from a site making many HTTP requests.

You might be wondering how you can improve your site performance in regard to page load speed and asset delivery. Here is my simple list of tips to help manage your content for performance:

- Serve only what the user needs at that moment; use an asynchronous delivery method for the rest.

- Be careful when deciding what content to show. If you do not need a content slider, don't use one. This feature might make a boss happy, but it can cause excess file download and site bloat.

- Combine as much of your CSS, JavaScript, and small images as possible into a single file. This means that you should be using sprite files for images and icons (consider using SpriteCow for image sprite generation—see www.spritecow.com/). You should also be combining your JavaScript into a single file, if possible.

- Do not autoplay videos, music, or similar media on page load. This saves on HTTP requests and the bandwidth you will be paying for when loading large media files.

- Do not be afraid to use a web font, but try to optimize these as much as possible. Google Web Fonts has an optimization service that enables you to create fonts that contain only the letters you need. If you are including a web font for some specific typography and you don't need the entire alphabet, don't force users to download an entire font they will not need.

SEO Considerations

Your search ranking has the power to make or break your website. The general rule of thumb is that if your site does not appear in the top three results on any given search, your site has almost no chance of being found. Getting your page to rank as the number 1 result for as many relevant searches as possible is essential to getting your site used by as many people as possible. It also saves you a considerable amount of money in any paid-search campaigns you are running.

The days of sitting on a domain for a few years and then keyword stuffing, adding massive internal site linking, joining a link-sharing group, and adding metatag overload are over. Thanks to new search algorithms that measure social media impact, the actual content on the page, correct grammar, the use of "natural speech," and the determined level of authority on a given subject for a topic, rising to the top of any search engine is now heavily dependent on the attention you give to your content.

Generally, if a site serves pages that are all images, with zero text content, those pages will be moved down in search results. The same holds true for sites that include images and then use empty alt tags or ones that read "logo" or "image here."

You need to strike a balance between descriptive text and useful, properly tagged images. You might wonder about the use of infograms because they are all images with text inside them, but ask yourself when the last time was that you viewed a page that was only an infogram, not a page describing the infogram along with it or an invitation to download it.

Maximizing your SEO will continue to be a balancing act between text and images. However, if you remember that you are building for the user and that you are the foremost expert on the material, you should do fairly well. Maintaining your expertise on a subject helps keep you at the top of the search pile.

If you have never done any SEO work, you can get started with the basics by visiting the Google Webmaster tools (https://www.google.com/webmasters/tools/) and the Bing Webmaster tools (www.bing.com/toolbox/webmaster). Both sites get you started on the little things you can do now to learn more. You can also find tools and services such as ScreamingFrog (http://www.screamingfrog.co.uk/) and Moz (http://moz.com/) to get moving in the right direction.

User Expectations

Every device quietly trains its user on how to use it. Many device manufacturers have design standards and design guides to help designers and developers create apps that match an overall theme or match the way the system flows.

For example, Android™ users know that a menu is almost always found by tapping an icon in the top-left corner of an app. They expect drop-down options and other application choices to be at the top of the application window. They also expect to use the Back button near the bottom of the device whenever they get lost or want to move back a screen.

iOS users, on the other hand, expect most menu and application options to be at the bottom of the app and look for Back buttons, edit buttons, and similar buttons near the top of the window or application.

Knowing the device demographic of your users can influence your design choices because different users will be trained to use their devices—and, thus, your site, in a specific way that makes sense to them. It would be ludicrous to build a site using design patterns that work best for Android users if the bulk of your traffic comes from users on iOS devices.

To learn about who is visiting your site, you can implement a tracking system such as Google Analytics (https://www.google.com/analytics). Google currently offers this service for free. The system allows you to not only gauge site traffic, but also get a glimpse into the devices, operating systems, and capabilities of users visiting your site.

To learn more about the design guides for Android, visit the Design section of the Android developer website (http://developer.android.com/design/index.html).

To learn more about iOS design, visit the iOS Design Resources (https://developer.apple.com/library/ios/design/index.html).

Now that you've learned how choosing the right content can make a difference, let's take a look at one of the hottest web topics, especially in regard to displaying content and site performance.

Discussing Content Sliders

Popular design trends over the last couple years have included landing pages that feature an extremely large hero or splash image with smaller call-to-action subsections or articles. This is a great way to use large text, bold imagery, and, of course, a large logo to help establish brand.

Not too long after that, the content slider or carousel made an appearance. The web went through a virtual love affair with this feature, and a modern-day "blink" or "marquee" element suddenly found a home again. In a way, this was great because it gave every manager in the marketing department a separate space to fill with the content they each felt was the most important. Looking at the content slider from a performance angle, however, this is a costly implementation: Instead of having to load one fairly large image, many more images are loaded. The overall page size increases. Figure 1.5 displays two websites: one without a content slider and one with a content slider.

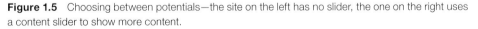

Figure 1.5 Choosing between potentials—the site on the left has no slider, the one on the right uses a content slider to show more content.

In terms of content value in relation to content sliders, the real question is, do they work? This is not an easy answer. Some sites use them with great success, yet others seem to have zero luck with them. Using a single hero image almost guarantees that a user will at least see it, whereas using a content slider creates the potential for users to see many images, but at the risk of not seeing more than one before they move on or scroll away. Getting the statistics on how your slider performs is crucial in deciding whether to use one. You can get this information using various analytic products, including Google Analytics. Just remember that some numbers might be artificially boosted if you have multiple links to the same place on a page. Enterprise solutions such as TeaLeaf from IBM (www.ibm.com/software/info/tealeaf/) give you an excellent way to track exactly what users did, when they did it, and whether they had any problems, or "thrashing," along the way.

Personally, I believe that a content slider acts exactly like a search engine. In this respect, you can think of your site as the "term" that was searched and then see each image in the content slider as the result pages of the search. Knowing that most users look at only the first three links on the first page of search results, how many users are willing to dig three or even five pages deep into the search results before clicking on one to get to the answer? This doesn't mean that something on page 5 doesn't have relevant information to users, but they might never get to see it. Worse, it might throw users off what they originally came to the site for. You're then left with a process that confuses users instead of giving them direct access to what they want.

The sites I see succeeding with content sliders are not necessarily selling themselves, but are serving fresh content that a user wants to access in order to properly use the site. As you think of and define your content strategy, keep this in mind.

Summary

Content affects your site in every way imaginable. You have learned what content consists of and various ways to generate content in a constructive manner.

You also learned the importance of delivering your message to the consumer and saw how choosing the right content to share is paramount in effective delivery and execution of your product, service, or site.

Finally, you learned that the content you decide to use affects load times, SEO scores, design layout, and the way you choose to expose content to the viewer.

CHAPTER 2

WHY MOBILE FIRST

You may have heard designers throwing around the phrase "mobile first." A developer might have said to you that implementation would have been ten times easier if only it had been mobile first. Or perhaps you have read Luke Wroblewski's 2009 blog post about mobile becoming the new medium. No matter where you have heard the phrase, starting mobile first is a sure-fire way to make sure that your design works for a majority of the people and that your most important details are front and center.

Viewing the Web

I remember the first television set we had growing up. It was probably only a 20-inch screen, but it came built into a cabinet that was so big and bulky that I couldn't move it by myself. It also had a knob that let you attempt to change channels manually, as well as a "fine-tune" knob that I used to try to improve the picture. I also remember that it was a color TV with another set of hidden knobs for adjusting the color, saturation, and contrast levels. In short, it was a marvel of modern technology at the time it was created.

Nothing was wrong with the TV: It served us well and let us tune into open-air broadcasts with our RF antenna. However, something extremely interesting happened. My older sister got a "portable" TV that she set up in her room. Even though her TV had roughly a 10-inch screen and was black and white, I could not help but be drawn to it. It was inferior to the large color-enabled beast in the living room in almost every way, but it was so small and light that I felt compelled to give it the time I had available for absorbing visual media.

I share this story because the device some people use to access the web might not be what some consider the "best" device for viewing the web. Devices that can view the web come in every shape and size.

> ## Tip
> iOS devices currently come in six different resolutions, ranging from 480x320 to 2048x1536. Thanks to the open nature of Android, hundreds of different devices and resolutions exist, from 240x320 to 2560x1600.

You might not know what device is being used to render a site (it could even be a smart watch), so you need to consider how you build sites and how you refer to various screen sizes.

For a while, designers and developers could refer to devices that had a mouse and clicked as a "desktop," whereas devices that featured a touchscreen (including tablets and phones) were "mobile." Then phones started having trackballs on them, and suddenly we had a touchscreen device that also had a mouse. Then people started using Bluetooth peripherals, and we soon had tablets that clicked. This situation continued to escalate, and soon laptops were released with touchscreens. Devices gained fold-away keyboards and screens that flipped around, phones plugged into tablets, and we saw the introduction of the "phablet," a mystery of device evolution for someone who simply could not part with the screen real estate of a tablet but still needed to make calls and send text messages.

With all these devices, functionality alone no longer determined whether a device was mobile or desktop. By the same token, the extreme physical screen size and the resolution of the phablets blurred, if not completely eliminated, the line that separated mobile device resolution from desktop resolution. Figure 2.1 shows a comparison of some popular device resolutions.

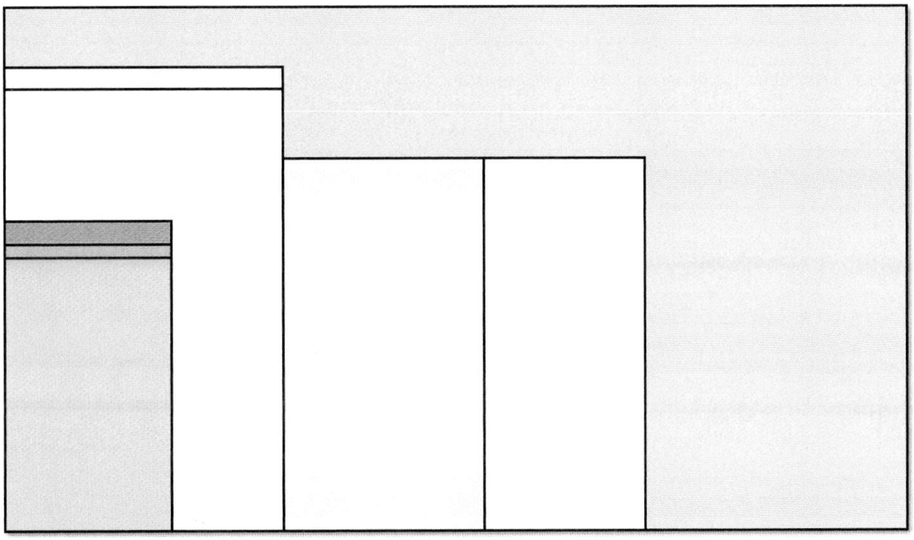

Color	Hex	Device	Pixel Resolution
Pink	#ffd9d9	HDTV	1920x1080
Light Blue	#d9e3ff	Kindle Fire HDX 7	600x960
Pale Yellow	#fff5d9	Laptop/Netbook	1366x768
Pale Green	#d9ffdd	iPad	1024x768
Yellow	#feff82	Nexus 7 (2013)	600x912
Salmon	#ff8282	Galaxy S4	360x640
Purple	#8b82ff	Moto X	360x592
Mint Green	#82ffc0	iPhone 5	320x568

Figure 2.1　Overlays of several popular screen resolutions when rendering a site.

How do we deal with such device diversity? Although some methods are currently circulating, I have stopped referring to devices by kind or type and instead group them by relative size. I generally use the following for my grouping:

- **0–479px:** Small
- **480–959px:** Medium
- **960–1,399:** Large
- **1,400+:** Extra large

Note that every project is different, and starting with breakpoints might not be the best solution. Many other designers prefer to build "in the browser" and create breakpoints when needed. The *need* is when your design no longer looks good and starts to look broken, stretched, stressed, or fractured.

Apple introduced what it called Retina screens. These screens were different from the standard screens that had been in use in monitors and other devices. They featured more pixels in a smaller space. In effect, this created a much sharper image with the availability of more pixels. Apple has always used a perfect ratio of 2 when adding pixels to the screen. This means that if a device was advertised as having a resolution of 640x1136 and a Retina screen, that device would actually render web pages as a device with a resolution of 320x568 would. Users then could use images that were twice as big as the rendered area, causing the image to be displayed with incredible sharpness and detail.

> ## Tip
>
> When dealing with high-pixel-density screens, you need to figure out the pixel ratio and then divide the device resolution by that ratio. The Samsung Galaxy S4 has a pixel ratio of 3, so if that device has an advertised 1080x1920px screen, it will display web pages the same way a 360x640px device would. A caveat to consider here is that a 360x640px image will appear fuzzy or blurry because of pixel doubling (or possible tripling). An image that is 1080x1920, on the other hand, will display with extremely sharp detail because it is confined to the smaller space and allows all available pixels to be used.

Hot on the heels of Apple, many other manufacturers wanted to get in on screens with high pixel density and coined similar marketing terms. Some, such as the qHD, contained a pixel ratio of 1.5 instead of 2. Some manufacturers do not care for creative terms and instead simply tout the total number of pixels and the sharpness of the display without pointing out the pixel ratio. These different methods of scaling have produced similar results, with increased sharpness of images and text, but with a wide range of effects on the amount of blur experienced when images and icons that are not twice the size display on such high-resolution devices. Figure 2.2 shows the difference in rasterized images that are not optimized for devices with a high pixel density.

I discuss displaying images properly in Chapter 9, "Responsive Images," but it is important to know about the way device resolution is marketed so that you know where to properly place a device in your device grouping.

Now that you've learned about sorting and dealing with screen sizes, it is time to consider what to keep in mind when starting a design, beginning with the smallest device size.

Figure 2.2 The image on the left appears with a high level of pixel distortion thanks to pixel doubling, whereas the image on the right appears with more clarity and sharper edges.

Considerations When Starting Small

The most difficult task I have come across when starting with a mobile design is convincing everyone that, even though it feels like I am taking their beautiful-bold design and cramming it into a plain box, everything will be all right. There is some truth to the fact that starting to design mobile first can feel a little uncomfortable, especially for anyone used to designing with large thunderbolt or cinema displays.

> ## Tip
> There is a trend suggesting that designs shouldn't be "mobile first" but rather "content first." As discussed in Chapter 1, "Content Matters," there is no denying the power of content in your design; however, a design should still be created mobile first—especially with regard to the user experience and development. Creating a CSS stylesheet with 20-30 breakpoints is not only difficult, time consuming, and confusing to write, but it is the incarnation of absolute chaos to manage.

The trick to starting out small is to keep some elements of your design or brand in play, maximize the use of colors and iconography, and keep the most important content up front and easily accessible to the user. Few things irritate mobile users more than taking a fully functional desktop site and then "trimming the fat" to give them only one or two options. If you would include a link, page, or feature on your desktop or "large" version of the site, you need a way to properly include it in a mobile or "small-to-medium" fashion.

This does mean that you need to start planning how everything is going to work at each of your site sizes. Depending on your interface design, this might increase your design and development time. The results will be worth it, though, and visitors will be happy to frequent your site or web application.

You might need to address some important areas early in the design process when starting mobile first:

- Site theme
- Site navigation
- Marketing images
- Site search

Let's break these down and discuss each of these issues and why they are important when starting a mobile-first design.

Site Theme

Your brand, site, colors, and logo likely have been developed over a series of carefully calculated tests, user feedback, and internal review. You also likely have spent time and resources enforcing the importance of your brand to your users. When designing small, brand preservation can be a somewhat challenging aspect in a limited space.

Some designers I have worked with suggest that, instead of getting wrapped up in worrying about how to shrink your entire logo or converting it to a smart object and crushing it into submission in Photoshop or Illustrator, you should strip it down to its essence in the same way you would if you were creating an application icon for a desktop or mobile app.

One of the beneficial aspects of Responsive Web Design is that, as the screen size increases, so does your ability to put more detail into your assets, including logos. Figure 2.3 shows a potential logo at different stages of implementation.

With the size of the logo taken care of, let's discuss how to reinforce a brand through a theme. Using a theme does not mean that you are restricted in your use of bright and vibrant colors, but it does mean that you should spend some time identifying what colors are important to your brand and what colors you are able to use as accent or alternate colors for your text, borders, buttons, and other elements.

I use a small palette of roughly 8 to 12 colors for my site theme. Figure 2.4 shows an example color palette I used on a project.

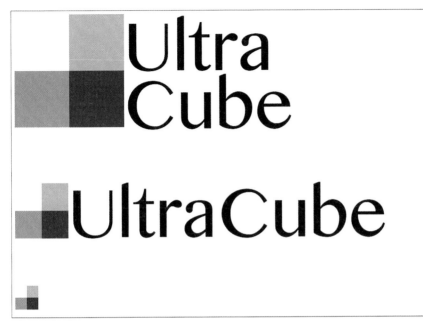

Figure 2.3 The evolution of a logo as it is displayed on different devices.

Figure 2.4 A sample palette with hex values and color descriptions displayed on each swatch.

By keeping my palette small, I can focus on the colors that mean the most to my brand, and I can train my users to quickly know what each color will do. For example, I use one color for all links or buttons that have a "forward" action, another color for all buttons that have a "backward" action, and another one for modal actions (such as launching overlays, video players, or in-page image galleries).

Note that your company, brand, or project might already have some web guidelines. If this is the case, you need to make sure that these guidelines can handle becoming fluid to match the various screens that will be viewing your site. If they cannot, you need to create a fluid version of the guidelines that can then be approved and used on your project.

This might feel limiting, and understandably so, but when starting small, you are building for brand reinforcement, speed, and usability. If users cannot use your website because 20 images need to be loaded first, or if users have to wait for layer after layer of parallax content to load without a good reason, they will leave—and be sure to tell as many people as they can about the horrible experience they had on your site.

Don't get me wrong, though: You should not be building three-color sites that are a soulless representation of what your brand means. You can feel free to use some eye candy, such as textures, patterns, and light layering. Just keep it within reason and make sure it benefits you and your users.

Site Navigation

Site navigation should never be an overlooked part of your design, especially in relation to small screens. New users need an intuitive way to find their way around your site, and returning users want an easy way to get back to where they were or to find the options they want. The situation can get complicated, however, because some returning users might accidentally end up in the new user camp because they are viewing your site on a mobile device for the first time.

Handling site navigation between screen sizes is a somewhat new practice, and as you browse the web, you can see how many different ways have been created to deal with it. Site navigation can generally be thought of as the menu of your site, so it is not uncommon to hear site navigation referred to as a "menu."

A menu is broken down into two elements, the button (or trigger) and the menu itself. The following is a list of common ways to display a menu button:

- The "hamburger," also known as the multiline menu
- The word *Menu* in text with or without a border
- Various icons or shapes
- Combinations of icon and text

Figure 2.5 shows examples of these popular menu styles.

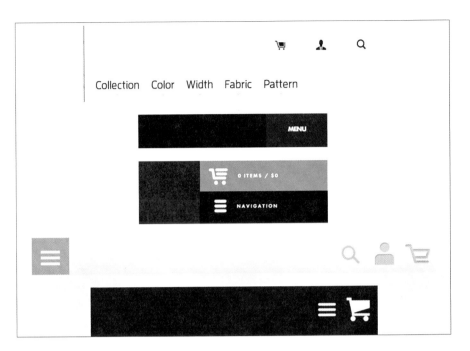

Figure 2.5   Multiple ways of displaying a button that triggers a menu.

After deciding what your menu button will be, you need to decide what will happen when it is triggered. As with menu buttons, you have several ways to display the menu element. The most common styles I see are usually drop-down (not select boxes, but either screen overlays or ones that move the page content down) or off-screen types that slide into view when the menu is triggered.

As long as you keep it consistent, any style of menu you choose can work, as long as you think about what will happen when your screen size changes.

Marketing Images

Whether you call it a hero, splash, zinger, bug, or call to action, at some point, you will be dealing with marketing images on your site. At first glance, you might approach this in a nonchalant manner, thinking that you can simply throw in an image and it will "shrink" to fit any size screen that is viewing your site.

To be blunt, thinking about images this way is wrong. Yes, your image might shrink down and, yes, the image might even look better when it shrinks and is viewed on devices that have a high pixel density. However, you might not be thinking about what happens to an image that contains text of a "standard font size" when it is compressed from 1400px wide to 320px wide.

Figure 2.6 demonstrates the rather unfortunate event that transpires when an image containing text is scaled down from 1920x1080px and rendered on a 480x270px screen.

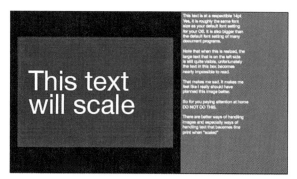

Figure 2.6   The text on the right side of the image becomes completely illegible when scaled down.

With proper planning, this now-illegible image would not have happened. When starting your design with the smallest screen first, you will find that your choice of art direction becomes an even more important part of the design process. Remember that your site content is not just text; your visual content is also critical. Figure 2.7 demonstrates how an image can change based on the screen viewing the image.

Figure 2.7   When viewed on different devices, the art direction of an image changes.

This issue is not bound to just text, either. Whether you are using a photograph of a group of people, an object, or a situation, what you decide to show at each screen size matters.

Site Search

The last area I bring to your attention in this chapter is one that developers often overlook on their own sites: site search.

Thinking about how mobile users go about their business, they generally have a short time span—and even shorter patience. Many do not have the time or willpower to dig through page after page of content to find what they want. If mobile users can't find what they are looking for in the first minute or less, there is a good chance that they will be gone from your site and might not return. Optimizing the way your site handles search should be another one of your top priorities.

Site search implementation is not yet an exact science, either, although many designs are getting closer to a solution that is universal in appearance. For now, most users know that an icon of a magnifying glass next to a field is the one they are searching for. If the field is absent and the icon appears to be on or part of a button, most users reason that they should attempt to click or tap the button, and a search form will appear.

One style of searching includes using a persistent field in either the header or the footer of the site, in either a static or fixed fashion. This is fairly common and can be quite successful in being "in your face" without being too pushy. The advantage of displaying your site search in this manner is that it is always available and in an easy-to-find location. The only caution I give you about this type of search is that when small-screen users turn their phones from portrait to landscape orientation, the search bar can take up a rather large area of now extremely precious screen real estate.

Another style of search that has become popular is an off-screen or "hidden" search area. These options are exactly what they sound like. For an off-screen approach, you need a menu that is off-screen (either the drop-down or slide-in variety). You then simply put the search field in the menu, making it accessible to the user. For a hidden search area, you add an icon, such as a magnifying glass, to your page. Then when the icon is tapped or hovered over, the search field appears and takes focus. The menu might appear through an action of sliding content out of the way when it appears, or it might be a menu or field that appears from behind other content. Nothing is necessarily wrong with either of these methods, but I must point out that some users might have issues using them because more thought is required to access them. Some users might also be afraid to tap on an icon if they do not recognize the symbol. Before committing to this in your design, build a prototype and do some group testing to make sure users understand how your search is accessed and used.

To visually summarize these search options, Figure 2.8 shows various search options in use.

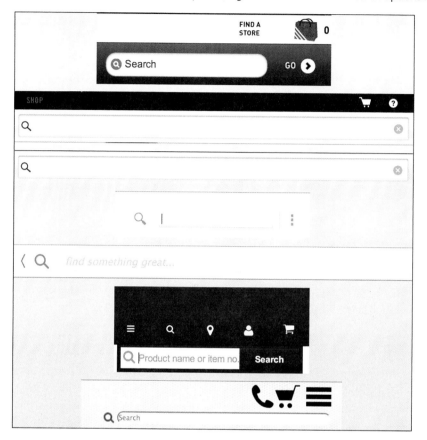

Figure 2.8   Examples of search options you can use on your site.

Summary

In this chapter, you learned why it is important to start thinking mobile first. You saw how you can leverage and enhance your content, brand, and even site interaction with mobile-first design. You learned about dealing with various screen sizes, including high-pixel-density devices that might report a higher resolution than they actually render your site in. You also learned about some common issues and pitfalls that can throw your design for a loop when starting with a mobile-first approach. Overall, starting mobile first can save you days of retrofit-ting and give you a clear path toward how you can expand your site as screen space becomes available.

CHAPTER 3

WORKING WITH GRIDS

A grid is not only useful when creating a graph or chart, it is also a great tool that you can leverage to arrange elements, align content to fit inside a region, and, more importantly, help your layout flex to meet the needs of the screen you are using.

Grid systems can be flexible and can change sizes to fit your layout needs by using gutters and widths set in percentages that shrink and grow as space is made available. On the other hand, they also can be very rigid, which makes them perfect for adaptive layouts.

Choosing a Grid

When first moving to a grid system, you might feel somewhat constrained. On one hand, it can be liberating to have something that gives your design a defined structure and aligns in near perfection when viewed on myriad screens. On the other hand, the idea that your design is no longer a free-flowing extension of yourself might leave you feeling like someone just tricked you into standing in a jail cell.

You should know right up front that although there will be some growing pains, using a grid doesn't have to end up as a prison sentence. For those who are concerned that, from now on, every design you create will become something henceforth referred to as "variations of a rhombus," know that you are limited only by the way you present your ideas.

If you have never used a grid system, you should ask yourself a few questions:

- Is this grid fixed or fluid?
- How "portable" is the system? Do I have to pull down an entire JavaScript library along with the styles to make the system work?
- Can this system integrate with other frameworks?
- Does it work with LESS?
- Does it work with Sass?
- Should I build my own?
- Does someone I know already use one?

> ## Tip
>
> Many JavaScript frameworks are popular today. These frameworks help developers get things done in a more convenient manner by offering plugins and shortcuts. Several libraries available for CSS offer shortcuts, pre-processing, post-processing, variables, and more that can help with web development projects. Among these, LESS, Sass, and Stylus are very popular. If you are constantly working with CSS files, look into these frameworks to improve your workflow.

Something else you should be keeping in mind while you design is that just because you have content that spans multiple columns doesn't mean that you absolutely need to fill 100% of the available space. If you did, you would end up building the "variations of a rhombus" that we discussed earlier. Using images in creative ways that might take up 3 3/4 columns is still a great option and a way to break up the symmetry of a design.

> **Tip**
>
> A grid is a guide—it is not an absolute. You should (and will) be able to display content in creative ways without breaking your site, as long as you plan ahead.

Now that you are ready to take a look at using a grid, it's time to view some of the grids and grid systems that you can download and get started with right away. Note that many different grid systems exist, and even more frameworks include a grid system. Before you commit yourself to using one in a project, spend some time doing some research and building some prototypes to test with. It might also do some good to consult your developers to see if they have an opinion about grids and implementation of a specific system.

Pure Grids

Pure, a popular CSS framework, aims to give developers and designers the tools they need to get the job done in an attractive, modular system. Pure Grids (http://purecss.io/grids/) is the system for creating the grid system you need. One of the most interesting parts of Pure Grids is that, instead of using a column number setup, it uses fractions. Pure Grids also works with both responsive and adaptive layouts and allows you to mix and match as needed.

Using Pure Grids is as easy as using the entire Pure library or including just the style sheet. You can also visit http://yui.github.io/gridbuilder/ to create your own grid system with custom breakpoints.

Bootstrap

Bootstrap is the popular framework created by Twitter. As you might have guessed, it also has a grid system. The grid system is included in the CSS, available at http://getbootstrap.com/css/. Here you will find a fluid grid system that scales up to a 12-column layout. It also includes LESS styles for you to use and modify as needed.

The Bootstrap library is a great place to get started when building prototypes, personal sites, or project sites.

Foundation

Foundation, by Zurb, is a project I have watched since the beginning. Zurb originally released some excellent modal/light-box and content slider solutions that I really enjoyed, so when Zurb decided to bundle its entire toolkit and release it to the masses, I was quite thrilled. Currently, Zurb allows the download of either components or the entire toolkit. The Grid (http://foundation.zurb.com/grid.html) is a component of the toolkit that you can download and use to create a fluid 12-column grid. Similar to other grid systems, you can offset columns, nest them, and customize them through mix-ins (note that these mix-ins are Sass based).

Gridpak

Gridpak (http://gridpak.com/), created by Erskine Design, has a wonderful site that generates a grid system based on your input. Using the generator is as simple as choosing the number of columns, the padding for your columns, and the gutter width between columns that you would like at a specific breakpoint. You then drag a slider to where you want the breakpoint and click a button. When you are finished creating breakpoints, you can download a zip file containing everything you need to get started, including the following:

- Demo HTML file
- Sample, development, and production CSS files
- PNG images of your grids that you can use as overlays in your favorite image editor
- LESS file (if you use LESS)
- SCSS file (for Sass developers)
- JavaScript plugin for toggling grid visibility

Gridpak is a great place to get started with grids—and if you make a mistake, it is easy to create a new grid and try again.

Golden Grid System

The Golden Grid System (http://goldengridsystem.com/) was created by Joni Korpi as an easy-to-use 18-column grid that aims to scale from small screens all the way up to screens with resolutions larger than 2560px wide. The Golden Grid System comes with the following as a download:

- Demo HTML file
- CSS file with comments and samples
- LESS file
- SCSS file
- JavaScript file that shows a baseline grid onscreen

Frameless (Adaptive)

The Golden Grid System is great for flexible responsive layouts, but adaptive users might want something with a little less flex. This is where Frameless (http://framelessgrid.com/) comes in. This system was also built by Joni Korpi as an option for designers and developers who do not care for percentages and just want a system that displays in a certain way between sizes. With a fairly straightforward setup, it includes a download that contains the following:

- LESS file
- SCSS file
- HTML template
- Photoshop template

Skeleton

The Skeleton (www.getskeleton.com/) system is based on the 960 Grid System. It uses similar concepts and layout, such as a 12-column system that easily resizes itself based on the amount of space available. Instead of focusing on a few media queries, Skeleton has built in quite a few to help you target specific devices.

From the main site, you can choose to download a Photoshop template or a zip file that contains the following:

- HTML demo file
- Three CSS files that contain basic styles, a grid, and media queries
- Sample images for your favicon and icons for iOS devices

Now that you have been introduced to some examples of grid systems, it is time to learn about actually using one.

Using a Responsive Grid

By now, you should be quite familiar with the phrase *responsive web design*, and you have probably seen an argument or two arise over the semantics of *adaptive layout* versus *responsive design*. If you have ever asked yourself what the difference is between the two, let me answer that for you. *Responsive* is elastic, stretchy, or flexible, whereas *adaptive* is fixed, static, or rigid in regard to a layout.

Fact

Ethan Marcotte coined the term *responsive web design* in 2010. Aaron Gustafson coined the term *adaptive web design* in 2011 and talked about it as another term for "progressive enhancement," mentioning that fixed layouts are mobile first and are part of the adaptive web design process. Since then, many debates have arisen over which layout method, responsive or adaptive, is better suited for the task of displaying websites on mobile devices. Rather than fuel the fire, I recommend you build a prototype of each layout method and see which one fits your style—and, more importantly, your users.

To help illustrate what it means to use a responsive grid, Figure 3.1 shows a responsive site that was built using a responsive grid on two different screen sizes.

Figure 3.1   A site built using a responsive grid stretches to fill the viewport.

At first, it might seem natural to start with a responsive grid. You load a template in Photoshop (or your preferred image rendering program) and then start moving bits of the site around, being sure to stay within the grid spaces and taking care to watch out for the spaces and gutters. Your design looks perfect, and you slice it or hand it off to a developer. Then you see the prototype, and your jaw drops. That is *not* what you designed.

Remember that, if you have been creating pixel-perfect designs, you will need to break that habit. This is responsive, elastic, or flexible design. If you are creating designs with images cut specifically to 320px, for example, and your breakpoint goes from 0 to 480px, you need to think about what happens when your design is viewed on a 480px screen. Figure 3.2 demonstrates what can happen when you have a design built for 320px viewed on a 480px device.

If a design has possible rendering issues, why would you even want to use a responsive grid? I am glad you asked. Using a responsive grid allows you to reflow content that would not normally fit on your screen, as well as deal with extreme site margin. Figure 3.3 shows a site that is centered at 960px but is viewed on a larger screen, leaving hundreds of pixels of site margin.

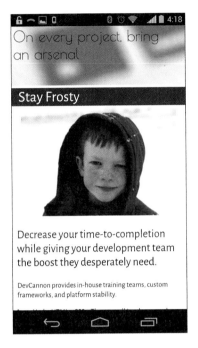

Figure 3.2 The image on the site is exactly 320px, making the margins look out of place between image and copy.

Figure 3.3 Without a responsive layout, the site looks small in comparison to the margins and doesn't take advantage of the available screen space.

With a responsive layout, you can take advantage of all the available screen space. It will take some getting used to, but you now have a magic canvas that shrinks and grows depending on the viewer of your art. You now have to think of how to best showcase your design, no matter what "canvas" users are applying your image to.

As for the image that doesn't quite fit when your design is between breakpoints, you can deal with that by adding a texture or background color or by using a responsive image technique to display an image that will fit the area.

Consider this quick list of pros and cons for using a responsive grid:

Pros:

- Uses all available screen space
- Allows content to reflow and stay within the bounds of column(s)
- Can be used with responsive image techniques to display images with chosen art direction on screens of different sizes

Cons:

- Requires increased effort to make sure a design will work when it stretches
- Can increase maintenance as the need to choose proper images is required
- Can have a steep learning curve when trying to wrap your head around a flexible design

Whether you are limited by the technology your developers are using or whether the design just does not come together when displayed in a flexible way, you might want to use an adaptive grid system.

Using an Adaptive Grid

As previously mentioned, an adaptive layout is based on columns with fixed widths that change with media queries for different screen sizes. For example, instead of creating a breakpoint at 480px, perhaps you would create one at 600px and create a fixed width of 320px for any device that views it. This could be used to center your design and then would display a pattern, tile, background, or texture in the margin around the site.

Adaptive grids can help mitigate the confusion and frustration when moving from pixel-perfect layouts to fluid ones. Although the approach can leave large swaths of screen space as empty margins, this can help designers get used to the idea of multiscreen development without tossing some of the traditional techniques they have used previously. Figure 3.4 shows what an adaptive layout looks like on a mobile device.

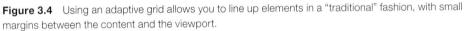

Figure 3.4   Using an adaptive grid allows you to line up elements in a "traditional" fashion, with small margins between the content and the viewport.

I have heard many people say that adaptive layouts feel outdated compared to the full-screen nirvana of a responsive design. In practice, however, I have found that, with proper planning, you seem to get less of the "80-pixel limbo" that can plague fluid designs when a device is at the extreme of a breakpoint and the site just looks awkward. You might also want to compare and contrast Figure 3.4 with Figure 3.2. Both figures feature the same site viewed on the same device; however, with the adaptive layout, small margins appear between the edges of the device viewport and the main content.

Another fear you might have when you design responsively is losing the ability to put elements exactly where you want them. When you start with a grid, it is extremely natural to want to put everything in a column. However, you will find that some items will not align or will look terrible when they are aligned. Figure 3.5 shows the header section of a site that is using an adaptive grid but has some elements placed with positioning.

Figure 3.5   The logo and various icons are placed with absolute positioning.

Consider this quick list of pros and cons for using an adaptive grid:

Pros:

- Gets you as close to pixel-perfect layouts as you are going to get with media queries
- Might be easier to understand and implement
- Avoids pixel limbo, when the design falls apart for devices at the extremes or at over-lapping areas of breakpoints

Cons:

- Can waste a lot of screen space with margins
- Can require more breakpoints to fill in the gaps

Best of Both Worlds

You don't need to draw a line in the sand and choose one style over another. In some cases, it makes good sense to actually combine both responsive and adaptive techniques in your design.

A design for small screens might use a fluid grid to help maximize the amount of space available, whereas a design for a large screen might opt instead for a fixed layout to help with asset delivery and display. As an example of what this can look like, Figure 3.6 shows a site as viewed from a small- and a large-screen device.

Figure 3.6   Responsive on the small screen, but adaptive on the large screen—the best of both worlds.

Summary

In this chapter, you learned that grid systems are a useful tool in your design arsenal that will help your design flourish on everything from small screen devices to large displays. Remember, the grid is not a cage—it is a tool to be leveraged and applied only when it fits the design and the user.

You have seen many examples of grids that you can use for learning, prototyping, and even integration into your projects.

You also learned that not all grid systems or designs need to be edge-to-edge responsive, but they can be contained in an adaptive design.

CHAPTER 4

DISPLAYING TABULAR DATA

When creating a new site or design, many times you can get caught up in making sure that the colors are just right or that the images have just enough treatment to tie everything together. It becomes so easy to get wrapped up in the nuances of creating or selling "the vision" that some tasks, such as displaying a table of data, become a last-minute priority. Previously, that was not much of a problem. You could simply throw data into a table, and either the screen was big enough to display the information or the user could scroll to see the entire table. When dealing with mobile devices, this is no longer the easy solution.

In this chapter, you learn some different approaches to dealing with tabular data and displaying data to users without relying on them having huge screens to see all the data.

Defining Tabular Data

You might already have an opinion of what qualifies as tabular data, and there are probably some aspects of it you haven't thought about. Many developers refer to tabular data as data that requires a table element to be displayed correctly. This is similar to invoices, receipts, and spreadsheet data. If you think about the web and all the various apps and sites you visit, I'll bet that most of them have some form of tabular data. It might not appear in a way you expect, though, and it might not even be wrapped in actual code that creates a table. The following discussion breaks down some of the form elements and data that you might use that I classify as tabular data.

Contact and Address Lists

Some designs are done so well that even though you know you are looking at a list (one that is even sortable, mind you), you feel like it is just the natural way to view data. Not all contact and address lists are created equal, and some are crafted so they do not even feel like a list.

Some lists are created just like a table; they have a header row and data directly under them. For example, you might find header columns of Name, Phone, and Address. Other lists use an image with a contact name as an overlay of the image. Even with radically different approaches, this data can still be considered tabular data.

Invoices and Receipts

This one almost goes without saying, but most printable or paper invoices and receipts are excellent examples of tabular data. They consist of data that is shown in rows and columns, with the intention of being easy to read and understand.

Whether you just picked up your groceries or are sending a client the latest invoice, the data that is displayed is in a name-value pair, an itemized listing, or even a label-input format.

Forms

On any given website used to purchase services or goods, users are required at some point to fill out a form. With luck, the form is designed with care, asking minimal questions while making very clear what it requires. Hopefully it includes fields that are considered "smart" by allowing users to enter their full name in one field instead of three or four separate fields. This is also a perfect example of tabular data. A group of input fields is aligned with, or hopefully at least near, matching labels. These fields might not actually be in a table, but the form is tabular data.

Recipes and Cards

Fitness sites, cooking sites, and blogs that display meals and recipes are great examples of tabular data. That pinch of salt, dash of brown sugar, and generous helping of love on a recipe site is also tabular data that helps you know exactly how much of each ingredient to use.

Some sites do not necessarily use a recipe but still contain tabular data. These sites use "cards," "boards," or "notes" to display various pieces of data, whether the person posted some data, a description of what a link contains, or even various embedded files or media.

Some applications, such as those that read RSS feeds, display news stories in a tabular fashion. Generally, these consist of an image, a headline, and a short clip of what the story contains. Many of them are even displayed in cards that fold, flip, or rotate away, showing more stories or items as they dance away from the screen.

Email Sites and Applications

The content of the email itself isn't very tabular, but the listing, sorting, and display options for each message is. Most email clients, sites, and applications list messages in rows with labels, names, and subject lines all neatly arranged, ready for you to summarize and decide whether to delete, read, or archive.

Working with Tabular Data

Now that you've seen some examples and patterns of tabular data, it is time to learn about how you can display forms and tables on mobile devices.

Displaying Forms

I'm going to start with something simple: the everyday input form. You might be familiar with input forms, but let's cover the different pieces that actually go into building the form. Each form generally consists of labels, input fields, and some type of submit element. Figure 4.1 shows a form as viewed on an Android device.

From Figure 4.1, you see that the form has multiple labels (Name, Address, Email, and Social Network). You can also see that several types of input are available (text field and a select or drop-down field). On the surface, this is a very usable form that would function as expected. This would definitely be the case for many desktop and laptop users, but many mobile users would not be able to accurately use the form without zooming in and out. Figure 4.2 demonstrates what happens on the same Android device when a text field is tapped and activated.

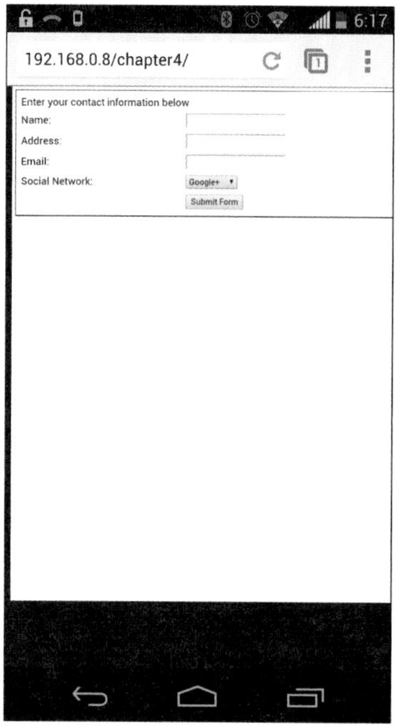

Figure 4.1   A contact form as viewed on an Android browser.

Figure 4.2   A field on the contact form is activated causing the onscreen keyboard to appear and the screen to zoom in.

Because the screen zooms into the field and the onscreen keyboard appears, the labels are no longer visible. This poses a major problem for users who want to fill out the form and not spend time memorizing what the label was for each entry field.

> ## Tip
>
> You probably thought labels were no longer needed because most devices support using the "placeholder" property. This looks great on paper and in design mocks, but in practice, this is a horrible idea that will confuse and irritate users, for one main reason: The placeholder disappears when the field is active. On a mobile device, the screen will zoom in to the field, the onscreen keyboard will appear, and the user will not be able to see what the placeholder was. If you want people to use your site, make sure you label each field clearly.

How can you overcome this labeling issue? It's actually simple. Make sure your labels are above the input fields. Figure 4.3 shows the same form, rebuilt to have labels shown above the input fields and viewed on a mobile device.

Figure 4.3   The label for the activated field is now visible, allowing the user to see what should be entered.

Now that the fields are looking great, what needs to be done when you have multiple forms that would normally appear side by side on a desktop? If you followed my recommendation in Chapter 3, "Working with Grids," you are hopefully already using a grid system. Listing 4.1 shows some markup of two forms using the Base grid framework (https://github.com/dutsonpa/base).

Listing 4.1   Showing Multiple Tables with Grid Classes in HTML

```
01 <div class="row clearfix">
02   <div class="col span_6 mo_full">
03     <table>
04       ...
05     </table>
06   </div>
07   <div class="col span_6 mo_full">
08     <table>
09       ...
10     </table>
11   </div>
12 </div>
```

As these forms are built, they will each take up roughly half of the available screen space. This is great for large-screen devices, but it still poses a problem for smaller devices. Luckily, we have already planned ahead. In lines 2 and 7 in Listing 4.1, you can see that I have added a class named mo_full. This is a utility class I have defined that bridges the gap in styles for a grid system that will display elements at 100% width on mobile screens. Listing 4.2 shows the media query and style for that class.

Listing 4.2   CSS for a Media Query and a Class

```
01 @media screen and (min-width: 0px) and (max-width: 479px) {
02   .mo_full {
03     width: 100%;
04     margin-left: 0;
05   }
06 }
```

By using a media query for the smaller-screen devices, I can make the elements take up the full screen. This does make users have to deal with a longer page, but for accessibility, this is a much better option than having them attempt to use fields in which only five or six characters are visible on each input field. Figure 4.4 shows the form viewed on a large-screen device and a small-screen device.

Now that you know how to deal with forms, it is time to look at dealing with actual tables.

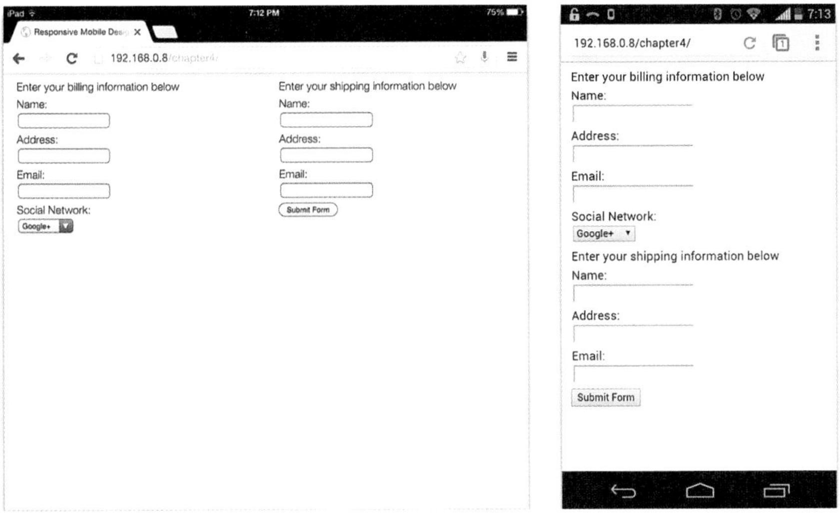

Figure 4.4 By using media queries, the forms can be moved to provide a better user experience on different devices.

Working with Tables

On the surface, tables seem like a nonissue. Their markup makes them flexible and already capable of shrinking and growing to fit the content. Because of this fact, developers have used tables to control layout by embedding multiple tables within each other. Most developers have since abandoned using tables for layout, but they still remain a problem on mobile devices.

Imagine that we had a table for song data that showed the ranking, weeks on chart, artist, album, and song title. It would fit well on a large-screen device, but on a small-screen device, it would quickly become a mess. Figure 4.5 shows this example on both a large-screen and a small-screen device.

How do we deal with this issue? Here are a few solutions:

- Build the table with CSS and then use media queries to change appearance.
- Build different tables and toggle visibility based on media queries.
- Swap out the table for a download button that links to a PDF file.

Using CSS to Change Appearance

You can build and display tabular data without actually using a table element. Instead, you can use some CSS to make it happen. By adding some media queries, you can then change the style or even hide some information to allow it to be viewed on a mobile device. Listing 4.3 shows the markup we will be using for the table.

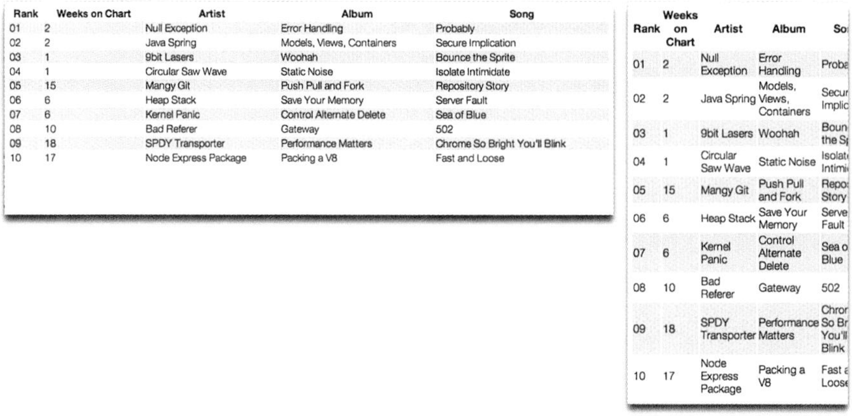

Rank	Weeks on Chart	Artist	Album	Song
01	2	Null Exception	Error Handling	Probably
02	2	Java Spring	Models, Views, Containers	Secure Implication
03	1	9bit Lasers	Woohah	Bounce the Sprite
04	1	Circular Saw Wave	Static Noise	Isolate Intimidate
05	15	Mangy Git	Push Pull and Fork	Repository Story
06	6	Heap Stack	Save Your Memory	Server Fault
07	6	Kernel Panic	Control Alternate Delete	Sea of Blue
08	10	Bad Referer	Gateway	502
09	18	SPDY Transporter	Performance Matters	Chrome So Bright You'll Blink
10	17	Node Express Package	Packing a V8	Fast and Loose

Rank	Weeks on Chart	Artist	Album	So
01	2	Null Exception	Error Handling	Proba
02	2	Java Spring	Models, Views, Containers	Secur Implic
03	1	9bit Lasers	Woohah	Boun the Sp
04	1	Circular Saw Wave	Static Noise	Isolate Intimi
05	15	Mangy Git	Push Pull and Fork	Repo Story
06	6	Heap Stack	Save Your Memory	Serve Fault
07	6	Kernel Panic	Control Alternate Delete	Sea o Blue
08	10	Bad Referer	Gateway	502
09	18	SPDY Transporter	Performance Matters	Chron So Br You'll Blink
10	17	Node Express Package	Packing a V8	Fast a Loose

Figure 4.5   The table is easily read on the large screen but is difficult to read on the smaller screen.

Listing 4.3   HTML Markup of a Table

```
01 <div class="table">
02    <div class="row clearfix">
03      <div class="title col rank">Rank</div>
04      <div class="title col weeks">Weeks on Chart</div>
05      <div class="title col artist">Artist</div>
06      <div class="title col album">Album</div>
07      <div class="title col song">Song</div>
08    </div>
09    <div class="row clearfix alternate">
10      <div class="col rank">01</div>
11      <div class="col weeks">2</div>
12      <div class="col artist">Null Exception</div>
13      <div class="col album">Error Handling</div>
14      <div class="col song">Probably</div>
15    </div>
16    <div class="row clearfix">
17      <div class="col rank">02</div>
18      <div class="col weeks">2</div>
19      <div class="col artist">Java Spring</div>
20      <div class="col album">Models, Views, Containers</div>
21      <div class="col song">Secure Implication</div>
22    </div>
23    ...
24 </div>
```

On line 1, you can see that a `div` element is used as a container and given a class of `table`. Lines 2, 9, and 16 show several `div` elements that define the rows of the table. These are designated by having the class row applied to them. Other common elements are the class of `col`, which signifies that the element will be used as a column, and the title of each column. Now that the HTML is in place, Listing 4.4 shows the CSS that makes the "nontable" work like a table.

Listing 4.4   CSS Used to Style a Table Without Using a Table Element

```
.alternate {background: #BFFFB3;}
.title {text-align: center;font-weight: bold;}

.col {
  border: 0px solid rgba(0, 0, 0, 0);
  float: left;
  -webkit-box-sizing: border-box;
  -moz-box-sizing: border-box;
  box-sizing: border-box;
  -moz-background-clip: padding-box !important;
  -webkit-background-clip: padding-box !important;
  background-clip: padding-box !important;
}

@media screen and (min-width: 0px) and (max-width: 479px) {
  .rank, .artist, .song {
    width: 32%;
    border-left-width: 0;
    padding: 0 1.5%;
    margin-left: 2%;
  }
  .weeks, .album {display: none;}
}

@media screen and (min-width: 480px) and (max-width: 959px) {
  .rank {
    width: 15%;
    border-left-width: 0;
    padding: 0 1.5%;
    margin-left: 2%;
  }
  .weeks {
    display: none;
  }
  .artist, .album, .song {
    width: 23.5%;
    border-left-width: 0;
    padding: 0 1.5%;
    margin-left: 2%;
  }
}
```

```
@media screen and (min-width: 960px) {
  .rank {
    width: 6.5%;
    border-left-width: 0;
    padding: 0 1.5%;
    margin-left: 2%;
  }
  .weeks {
    width: 15%;
    border-left-width: 0;
    padding: 0 1.5%;
    margin-left: 2%;
  }
  .artist, .album, .song {
    width: 23.5%;
    border-left-width: 0;
    padding: 0 1.5%;
    margin-left: 2%;
  }
}
```

Notice that the styles have been put in place from smallest to largest. This follows the pursuit of mobile first, and it allows us to use some styles as a global setting and then fine-tune the styles in each media query. Figure 4.6 shows how the table is rendered on two different screens.

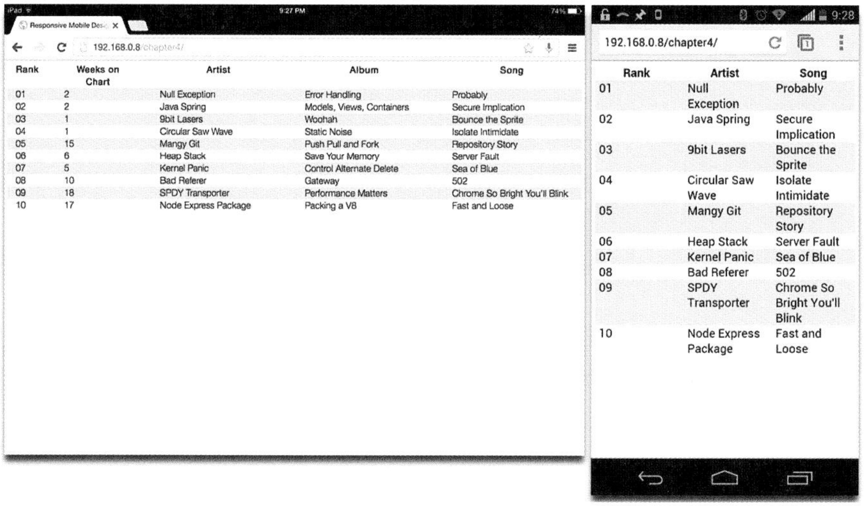

Figure 4.6   The table changes appearance based on the device viewing it.

A more complex solution that builds on this technique is to create a menu that allows the user to change which columns are shown in the table at various screen sizes. This gives users access to the entire table, albeit not all the data at the same time.

Building Multiple Tables

Adjusting the table layout with CSS alone might not solve the problem, though, and it might be better to use an entirely different table that has been designed to fit various screen sizes. If you find this is the case, you can build multiple tables and then apply classes that will show and hide them using style in your media queries.

In Listing 4.5, three tables are built in HTML. Listing 4.6 shows the CSS to make each appear for various screen sizes.

Listing 4.5   Building Tables in HTML

```
<table class="small">
  <tr>
    <th>Name</th>
    <th>Username</th>
    <th>Extension</th>
  </tr>
  <tr>
    <td>Ronald Crimson</td>
    <td>r.crimson</td>
    <td>9001</td>
  </tr>
  <tr>
    <td>Breck Champ</td>
    <td>b.champ</td>
    <td>9009</td>
  </tr>
  <tr>
    <td>Ryan Timberland</td>
    <td>r.timberland</td>
    <td>9004</td>
  </tr>
</table>
<table class="medium">
  <tr>
    <th>Name</th>
    <th>Username</th>
    <th>Extension</th>
    <th>Department</th>
  </tr>
  <tr>
    <td>Ronald Crimson</td>
    <td>r.crimson</td>
    <td>9001</td>
    <td>Development</td>
  </tr>
  <tr>
```

```
      <td>Breck Champ</td>
      <td>b.champ</td>
      <td>9009</td>
      <td>Design</td>
    </tr>
    <tr>
      <td>Ryan Timberland</td>
      <td>r.timberland</td>
      <td>9004</td>
      <td>Marketing</td>
    </tr>
  </table>
  <table class="large">
    <tr>
      <th>Name</th>
      <th>Username</th>
      <th>Extension</th>
      <th>Department</th>
      <th>Manager</th>
    </tr>
    <tr>
      <td>Ronald Crimson</td>
      <td>r.crimson</td>
      <td>9001</td>
      <td>Development</td>
      <td>Ned Harokonnen</td>
    </tr>
    <tr>
      <td>Breck Champ</td>
      <td>b.champ</td>
      <td>9009</td>
      <td>Design</td>
      <td>Tino Downton</td>
    </tr>
    <tr>
      <td>Ryan Timberland</td>
      <td>r.timberland</td>
      <td>9004</td>
      <td>Marketing</td>
      <td>Garth Spaceman</td>
    </tr>
  </table>
```

You can see in Listing 4.5 that three tables are built and given classes of `small`, `medium`, and `large`. By using the CSS in Listing 4.6, we can change when these tables will be displayed.

Listing 4.6   Media Queries Used to Show and Hide Elements at Different Sizes

```
@media screen and (min-width: 0px) and (max-width: 599px) {
  .medium, .large {display: none;}
}
@media screen and (min-width: 600px) and (max-width: 959px) {
  .small, .large {display: none;}
}
@media screen and (min-width: 960px) {
  .small, .medium {display: none;}
}
```

Because we are using CSS to show and hide tables based on the size of the screen, this technique is similar to the method of creating and modifying a table with CSS.

> ## Warning!
>
> Building elements such as tables multiple times and then hiding them with CSS does not stop the items from being requested and downloaded by the browser. If you create three versions of a table that you want to be displayed at different sizes, all three tables will be downloaded by the user. Depending on the table structure and elements you are sending to the user, you can cause excessive overhead and make many requests that do not need to happen. You should create different versions of elements or tables only as a last resort. If you absolutely have to do it, try to minimize how many versions you will be creating. Note that users with disabled CSS, screen readers or similar assistive devices, and content scrapes will also receive all the data and might regard it as duplicate, excessive, or just plain irritating.

Using a Download Link

If you cannot display your table in a minimized fashion, you might want to forgo applying any styles and instead swap out the table altogether for a link to a downloadable version of the data. This is just like creating multiple tables: You create your table as usual and then change the visibility of the table by using a media query in your CSS. Listing 4.7 shows the HTML code used to create a table and the download button area.

Listing 4.7   Building a Table and Download Button in HTML

```
01 <div class="showmo">
02   <a href="directory.pdf" class="button">
03     Download the directory
```

```
04  </a>
05 </div>
06 <table class="nomo">
07   <tr>
08     <th>Name</th>
09     <th>Username</th>
10     <th>Extension</th>
11     <th>Department</th>
12     <th>Manager</th>
13   </tr>
14   <tr>
15     <td>Ronald Crimson</td>
16     <td>r.crimson</td>
17     <td>9001</td>
18     <td>Development</td>
19     <td>Ned Harokonnen</td>
20   </tr>
21   <tr>
22     <td>Breck Champ</td>
23     <td>b.champ</td>
24     <td>9009</td>
25     <td>Design</td>
26     <td>Tino Downton</td>
27   </tr>
28   <tr>
29     <td>Ryan Timberland</td>
30     <td>r.timberland</td>
31     <td>9004</td>
32     <td>Marketing</td>
33     <td>Garth Spaceman</td>
34   </tr>
35 </table>
```

Note the class of `showmo` that I have applied to the `div` element on line 1. This class is named `showmo` because it triggers the element to *show* on *mobile* devices. A similar class, `nomo`, has been applied to the table element on line 6. The `nomo` class is used to hide elements, or *not* display on *mobile* devices. Without applying some styling, both elements would be visible on the page. Listing 4.8 shows the media queries and styles applied to the `showmo` and `nomo` classes that toggle the visibility of the table and download button. I have also included the styles that create the button.

Listing 4.8 Styling a Button and Using Media Queries to Show and Hide Elements

```
a.button {
  width: 90%;
  margin: 0 auto;
  height: 40px;
```

```
    line-height: 40px;
    background: #09CC00;
    display: block;
    text-decoration: none;
    text-align: center;
    color: #fff;
    font-size: 125%;
    font-weight: bold;
    border: 2px solid #057300;
    text-shadow: 1px #333;
}
@media screen and (min-width: 0px) and (max-width: 479px) {
    .nomo {display: none}
}
@media screen and (min-width: 480px) {
    .showmo {display: none;}
}
```

The styling is rather minimal because the only time the download button should be shown is when the width of the device is less than 480px. Figure 4.7 shows the page viewed on a phone and on a tablet.

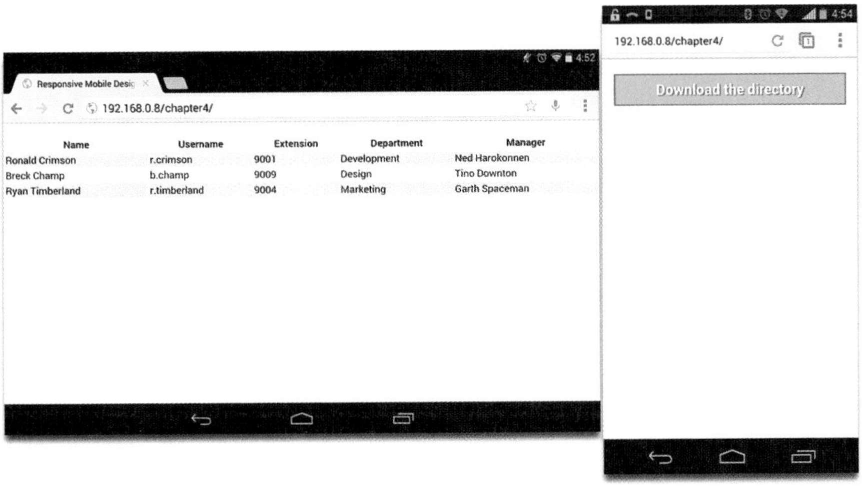

Figure 4.7   The table is visible and accessible on most tablet- and laptop- or desktop-size devices but is replaced with a download button for smaller-screen devices.

Summary

In this chapter, you learned that tabular data does not always require the use or markup of table elements. You also learned that you have options for displaying tabular data, including changing the styling of the table, adding multiple tables to your page, and even removing the table and replacing it with a link to a file.

CHAPTER 5

WORKING WITH MEASUREMENT VALUES

From creating a layout to working with line heights and font sizes, at some point you will need to use a measurement value. Even if you are already using a favorite measurement, another value might be a better fit for your current project.

In this chapter, you learn about the various options available for measurement, including pixels, percentages, em units, and more.

With so many devices in use today, what is the right value to use? Should you be using pixels for everything? What about em units? Well, it turns out that many different types of measurement values are available.

CSS3 introduced some new measurement values that actually have some decent support in today's modern browsers. Although this is welcome news for the future, it might leave you scratching your head, wondering why the design that looked so good on your computer and mobile devices looks broken and malformed on some of your friend's devices.

Let's look at the following measurement values and learn more about them:

- Pixels
- Percentages
- Em units
- Rem units
- Viewport units

Using Pixels

Odds are, you are familiar with pixels as a measurement value. For my own setup, I have Photoshop set to use pixels as the default measurement unit.

Pixel values are also a common measurement when it comes to setting up CSS values. Take a look at the following snippet:

```
.logo {
  width: 180px;
  height: 40px;
}
```

The values for the width and the height are set in pixels. These absolute units are great for dealing with static-sized elements, such as images, and pixel-perfect layouts.

Pixels are comfortable, classic, and still widely used. So what are the problems with using pixels? For one thing, a pixel is not always the same size. As Scott Kellum pointed out in an article on A List Apart (http://alistapart.com/article/a-pixel-identity-crisis/), it can be difficult to narrow down some pixel values, especially in regard to physical device pixels. Some of this is attributed to the fact that pixels are not always square; in addition, with various levels of pixel density on various mobile devices, pixel sizes are not the same physical size. Does this mean you shouldn't use pixels? No—it just means you need to be careful with how you use them. This is especially the case when working with mobile devices. If you are new to styling designs in CSS, starting with pixel values gives you a good start because it is a backward-compatible approach, and newer browsers will compensate most measurement values.

The iOS Safari browser provides a prime example when it comes to layout and design with pixels. When a developer builds a design and does not set the device width in an HTML `meta` tag, iOS browsers assign the viewport width to 980px. Be aware that this is not the number of device pixels, but the simulated pixel value of a page. This is generally a fairly safe size; however, if you have a website that is built at 1140px, the browser no longer shows you the site contents. This is because the simulated 980px is less than the 1140px you might have coded for. Figure 5.1 demonstrates how a page renders on an iPad when this is the case.

As you can see from Figure 5.1, the site is not fully displayed. The view on the iPad shows some text visible on the right that might prompt a user to pan or swipe over to it. The zoom level is not changed on the iPad, so only 980 pixels are shown.

Figure 5.1   When viewed on an iPad (left) in landscape, the navigation is not visible and the main text is cut off, forcing the user to zoom out to see the entire page. Viewed on an Android phone (right), even less of the site is visible.

The phone, however, has quite a problem: Not even 980px of the site are shown. Instead, the phone zooms in to attempt to make the site legible on the phone. Chapter 6, "Using Media Queries," deals with this particular issue, but for now, you can see that using pixels as the only form of measurement has inherent issues when it comes to site layout.

Using Percentages

Percentages are commonly used to adjust various element layouts and font sizes in CSS. Percentages are part of the magic that makes grid systems work and one of the leading causes of web developers inventing new words that make sailors blush and creatively express frustration.

This is because percentages have a somewhat abstract nature. You already know that 100% of an area adds up to all of it. What you might not realize is that, depending on your `box-model`, throwing a 1px border on both sides of an element that is using a style of `==width: 100%==` does not take up 100% of the available space; it actually takes up 100% + 2px of the available space.

> ## Tip
>
> The "standard" box model takes into account the element padding, borders, and assigned width to determine the actual space an element will take up. For example, an element with a 960px width, a 1px border, and 10px of padding will actually take up 982px of space (960 + 2px + 20px). The 2px comes from 1px on each side. The 20px of extra space comes from 10px of padding on each side. This can be extremely frustrating for those new to CSS. Luckily, you can change the way the box model is rendered on your site by changing the styles in your CSS. By adding **`box-sizing: border-box`**, you change the calculations to no longer include padding and borders as part of an element's width. For style prefix information, as well as browser compatibility, visit https://developer.mozilla.org/en-US/docs/Web/CSS/box-sizing.

Another easy-to-miscalculate issue that can occur is using percentages on child elements. A child element is a nested, or included, element. If there were a `<div>` element that contained a `<p>` element and an `<img>` element, the `<p>` and `<img>` elements would be child elements. Take a look at the following HTML snippet:

```
<body>
<header>
    <img src="images/logo.png" alt="my logo" />
    <nav>
      <ul>
        <li>Home</li>
        <li>About</li>
      </ul>
    </nav>
    Text in the header
  </header>
  <section>
    <p>Working with percentages</p>
  </section>
  <footer>
    <p>Text in the footer</p>
    <p class="special">Special footer text</p>
  </footer>
</body>
```

Now I add some styles to it using percentages:

```
body {
  font-size: 100%
}
header {
  font-size: 80%
}
nav {
  font-size: 150%
}
section {
  font-size: 100%
}
footer {
  font-size: 80%
}
.special {
  font-size: 80%
}
```

Those with experience in CSS should be able to spot some potential problems with the layout and styles that will be rendered onscreen. Figure 5.2 demonstrates how the percentages are applied and how they affect the rendering of text on a page.

Figure 5.2   Child elements inherit percentages, making some text appear smaller than originally designed.

Because of how percentages apply to all child elements, the text in the footer is originally displayed at 80% of the default font size; however, the "special" text is displayed even smaller. In fact, it is displayed at 80% of the original 80%. This type of mistake can be compounded by more child elements and by adjusting the font size for an element that is a container.

Another area that might be easy to miss is the size of the text in the navigation area. Even though it looks bigger than the surrounding text, it is not being displayed at 150% of the default text size; instead, it is being displayed at 150% of the 80% that the `header` element was set at.

To simplify, percentages will compound when used from parent to child element, making it difficult to track the actual size applied based on where the element exists in your HTML structure.

It might look like percentages are a terrible idea and should never be used (especially in regard to font sizes). However, you can use them safely as long as you remember to avoid nesting them. If you have no alternative but to nest them, make sure you do your calculations properly so that you aren't surprised by the resulting percentage.

When I use percentages on font sizes, I set the base font size on the body element and then use classes to change the font size in a given element instead of in container elements. The following snippet shows how to accomplish this in CSS:

```
body {
  font-size: 14px;
}
.small {
  font-size 80%;
}
.normal {
  font-size: 100%;
}
.big {
  font-size: 150%
}
.large {
  font-size: 200%
}
.massive {
  font-size: 300%
}
```

By using classes to adjust the font size, I can change any element, including using `span` elements to change the size of single words or sentences.

If you do not want to use percentages but would like to use another type of measurement that can help with responsive text, you can use the `em` unit.

Using Em and Rem Units

You've seen that pixels are absolute measurements and percentages are taken from context. `em` units are another way to scale content based on context.

`em` units have quite the history, including being set as the value of the height of the letter *M* in a given font. Now however, 1em is equivalent to one unit of the parent element font size.

This means that if you have a `section` element that is set at a font size of 16px and it contains a `p` element set at 1em, the `p` element will have a font size of 16px.

> ## Warning
>
> You might have heard that if a font size is not set on an element, that 1em will always be 16px. This is usually a safe assumption, but it is not always true. Not only do users have the ability to change the default font size displayed in their browser, but the browser itself could be using a different font size as the default setting. This could seriously affect your design and the way your fonts display. When dealing with the `em` unit, you can "reset" the parent element by applying a font size directly to that element, to ensure that any child elements will display `em` units as expected.

Remember the example shown for a potential problem when using percentages? It just so happens that `em` units are prone to the same behavior. This means that if you find yourself nesting any elements and attempting to apply a new `em` style to them, the resulting size will be based on the currently applied styles and not the base or root style.

Imagine that a parent element set at 16px has a child element set at 0.8em, and that has another element that is also set at 0.8em. The second element will not be displayed at 0.8em; instead, it will be displayed at 0.8em of 0.8em, or 0.64em of the original parent. Figure 5.3 helps you visualize how this works.

Luckily for us and the age we live in, we have a solution for dealing with nested `em` units: the "root `em`," or `rem` unit.

The `rem` unit was introduced as part of the CSS3 specification. It traverses back through the DOM tree to the `html` element for use as the base unit of measurement. If you are unfamiliar with DOM traversal, the simple explanation is that whatever size is assigned `html` will be the base unit of measurement used. This saves you from dealing with additive values and seemingly confusing sizes.

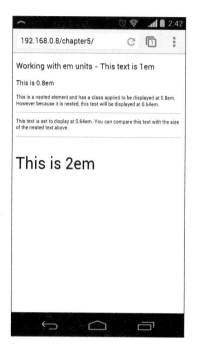

Figure 5.3   Just as you saw with percentages, em units are additive and can have an unexpected effect on layout.

As far as browsers go, support for the `rem` unit is very good. The following is a list of supported browsers:

- IE9+
- Firefox 3.6+
- Safari 5.0+
- Opera 11.6+
- iOS Safari 4.0+
- Android Browser 2.1+
- Blackberry Browser 7.0+
- Opera Mobile 12.0+
- Chrome for Android 32+
- Firefox for Android 26+
- IE Mobile 10+

With almost all current browsers supported (and even quite a few legacy ones), you can use `rem` units on almost any design. Be sure to check your site analytics for users who might be using an unsupported browser so that no one is left with a broken and unusable site. If you find that you must offer support for legacy devices, it might be best to convert to using calculated pixel values for your measurement values.

Figure 5.4 shows how using `rem` units can fix the problem that using `em` units can cause.

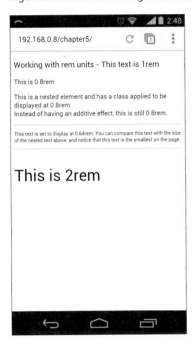

Figure 5.4 By using `rem` units, nested elements no longer calculate in an additive way.

Viewport Measurements

Now you know that pixels are very finite but they also might not mean the same thing on every device. You also know that percentages and `em` and `rem` units can be somewhat unpredictable when it comes to working with layout and font sizes. There has to be a better solution for working with screen measurements.

Viewport measurements are the answer you have been looking for. You can use four measurement values in your CSS: `vw`, `vh`, `vmin`, and `vmax`.

When working with `vw` and `vh`, keep the following in mind:

- 1vm = 1% of viewport width
- 1vh = 1% of viewport height

For working with more global settings, you might want to switch to using `vmin` and `vmax`:

- 1 `vmin` = 1vm or 1vh, whichever is smallest
- 1 `vmax` = 1vm or 1vh, whichever is largest

To use these in your styles, you need to assign them to an element or class. The following snippet shows how to do this:

```
.large {
 font-size: 5vw;
}
.small {
  font-size: 3vh
}
```

Remember that, because the units are based on either the width or the height of the viewport, they change when the screen is resized. This can cause interesting side effects, such as making the `.small` class just mentioned become as large as, if not larger than, the `.large` class when displayed on wide screens. Figure 5.5 demonstrates this.

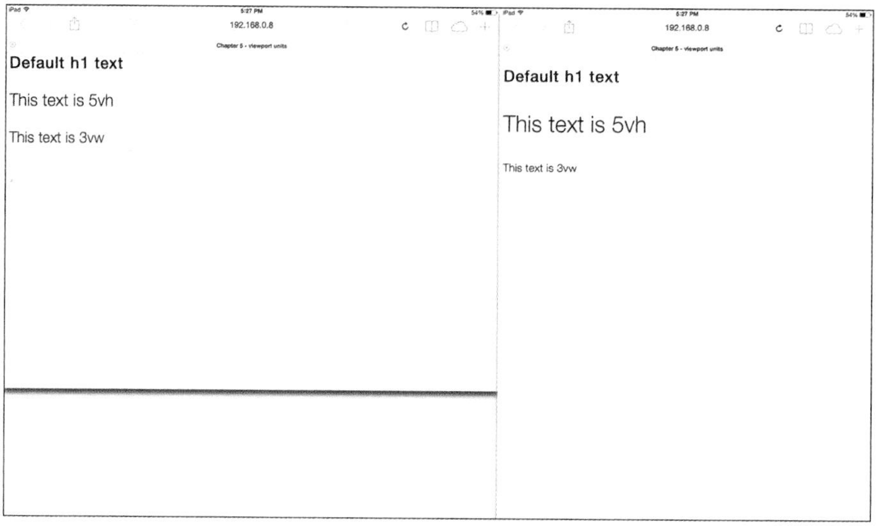

Figure 5.5   In portrait orientation, the text appears to match the class names; in landscape orientation, the text appears to be almost the same size.

> **Tip**
>
> Viewport units sound almost too good to be true—but they do have some drawbacks. For example, IE 9 uses vm instead of vmin. This can cause some added complexity to your styles and browser compatibility. Another problem is that, if not properly managed, some elements might get so small that the text will become completely illegible. Another problem is that not all browsers will trigger the font changes on screen size. In those cases, you need to either reload the page or trigger a "paint" event.

The text size might be a little tricky to line up, but when working with elements, the measurement is much simpler to understand. To see it in action, the following is some HTML markup that will be used to create a section for text and a section for a sidebar:

```
<div class="main">
 <p>
    This element is inside of an element that has been given a size of
    70vw
  </p>
</div>
<div class="sidebar">
  This is a sidebar that is 25vw
  <ul>
    <li>Item 1</li>
    <li>Item 2</li>
    <li>Item 3</li>
  </ul>
</div>
```

The following is the CSS that makes the layout work responsively:

```
.main {
  width: 70vw;
  float: left;
}
.sidebar {
  width: 25vw;
  margin-left: 75vw;
}
ul {
  margin: 10px 0 0;
  padding: 0;
}
```

I have floated both elements and given the .main element 70vw (remember, that is roughly 70% of the screen). I have given the .sidebar element a width of 25vw (again, 25% of the screen), and I have used a CSS style to adjust the left margin 75vw to help create a gutter that will be used to separate the content of each element. I have applied the styles to the `ul` element to reset the styles on that element. Figure 5.6 shows this site viewed on a tablet and a mobile phone.

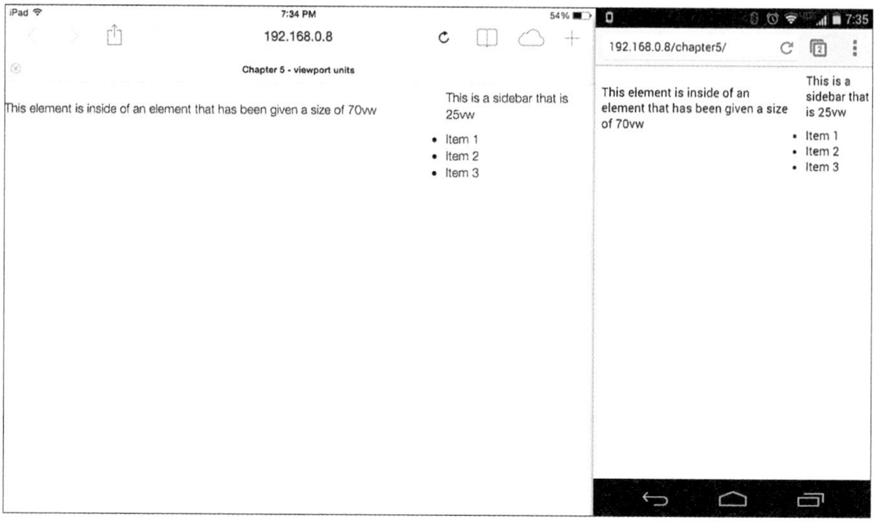

Figure 5.6   As viewed on both an iPad (left) and a Moto X (right), the site adjusts itself to fit the screen, per the `vw` measurement units.

Whether you decide to use the viewport measurement units on elements, buttons, or your text size, knowing what supports it is important. Note that you want to avoid some values, such as `vmax`, because they are poorly supported. The following is a list of supported browsers:

- IE 9+ (IE 9 uses `vm` instead of `vmin` and, like IE 10, does not support `vmax`)
- Firefox 19+
- Chrome 20+ (20–25 do not support `vmax`)
- Safari 6+ (6.0 does not support `vmax`)
- Opera 15+
- iOS//Mobile Safari 6+ (6.0–7.0vh units exhibit odd behavior)
- Android Browser 4.4
- Blackberry Browser 10+ (10.0 does not support `vmax`)
- Opera Mobile 16+
- Chrome for Android 32+
- Firefox for Android 26+
- IE Mobile 10+ (10.0 does not support `vmax`)

Summary

In this chapter, you learned that you can use several units of measure on both font size and elements. Some measurement units, such as pixels, can be unforgiving and are not suited for fluid and flexible type. Other units, such as percentages and em units, can be used on most browsers and offer flexibility in font size as long as they are carefully used in regard to their additive nature.

Whether you are designing for the future or you only have clients that use legacy browsers, you now understand how you can use sizes with layout and styles to provide an efficient solution that works.

CHAPTER 6

USING MEDIA QUERIES

Media queries have a history in CSS2 as a way to specify which styles are applied to different media. Originally, these attributes were setting `media="screen"` and/or `media="print"` when defining the styles for your site and printer to render the page.

The curious and beneficial path that today's media query is heavily involved in is allowing styles to be applied based on the width of the screen viewing the site. This does not mean that width is the only expression you can use; other expressions, such as color depth, pixel density, and even the aspect ratio, can also be used with media queries.

If you have ever dabbled in coding HTML, you have undoubtedly seen a call to a CSS file that has looked similar to the following:

```
<link rel="stylesheet" type="text/css" href="/style.css" media="screen">
```

This one-line snippet is a reference to a file (in this case, `style.css`) that will be called when the site is rendered on a "screen." A similar line of code could also be made to apply styles to a printer, as follows:

```
<link rel="stylesheet" type="text/css" href="/print.css" media="print">
```

If you are not one to dabble with HTML code, but you'd perhaps like to take a look inside CSS files, you might remember seeing some code that looks like the following:

```
@media print {
  body {
    font-family: Helvetica, Arial, sans-serif;
    color: #000;
  }
}
```

You might have recognized this code snippet as a basic style setup for a printer. And believe it or not, this is actually a media query. It is probably not what you think of when you hear about media queries, but it is a prime example of what they are and how they work.

The popular media queries that power responsive and adaptive websites today are rooted in styles that are applied based on screen dimensions and pixel density. For these to work properly on mobile devices, a `meta` tag must be used so that the size of the screen can be properly identified and used.

The Viewport Meta Tag

In Chapter 5, "Working with Measurement Values," you learned that pixels are not always measured the same, especially when it comes to mobile devices. The `viewport` meta tag was created to give developers control over how a page displays on a device and to help deal with small screens.

Mobile Safari was the first to implement this tag. Other browsers have been quick to implement support as well, allowing it to be used on most, if not all, modern browsers.

The `meta` tag (or element) consists of the element itself and two attributes. The `name` attribute informs the browser of the type of meta element this is. The second attribute, `content`, is filled with data that the browser uses to determine how to render the page inside the viewport of the browser.

An empty `viewport meta` tag looks like the following:

```
<meta name="viewport" content="">
```

To make the browser do something with this tag, you need to put some information into the content attribute. Table 6.1 lists the properties you can use inside the `viewport` meta tag:

Table 6.1   Description of Properties and Values of the `viewport` Meta Tag

Property	Description	Values
`width`	Sets how wide you want the viewport to be. You can use either a pixel value or `device-width`, to allow the device to set the width to match the reported screen size by the browser.	`320` or `device-width`
`Initial-scale`	Defines how zoomed in the page should appear. A value of `1.0` displays the page at 100% of the standard zoom; `1.5` shows it at 150%.	`1.0`, `2.0`
`maximum-scale`	Determines the maximum amount the viewport can be zoomed in. Setting this limits pinch-zooming by the user.	`2.0`, `8.0`
`minimum-scale`	Determines the minimum amount that the viewport can be zoomed out. Setting this limits pinch-zooming by the user.	`0.25`, `3.0`
`User-scalable`	Determines whether the user is allowed to zoom. The default value is `yes`; if it is set to `no`, the user is not allowed to zoom in on anything.	`no`

Tip

Allowing users to zoom is recommended because many users will want to zoom to read text, get a closer look at a picture, or even "reformat" the layout to ignore sidebars or ads. For a web app, however, you might want to disable zooming because it could make your application hard to understand or use. If you decide to limit a user's ability to zoom, make sure your design uses large text and buttons to make up for the limitations on accessibility that you have imposed.

Now that you have seen some of the possible settings, you might already be thinking that, by setting the width and possibly the scale values, you can lock users into the perfect view of your site. Before you get too carried away, remember that a pixel might not be what you think it is.

Because of the variety of devices, screen resolutions, and pixel densities, the following is the recommended `viewport` meta tag to use:

```
<meta name="viewport" content="width=device-width, initial-scale=1.0">
```

Using this meta tag, you allow the device viewing the page to set the width based on the number of pixels it reports available to the browser and still allow users to change zoom settings, if they wish. To illustrate this, Figure 6.1 demonstrates how a site appears based on the inclusion of the tag.

Figure 6.1　The missing meta tag can cause significant problems that might be hard to see, such as missing navigation (left). With the tag included, the site appears zoomed out, with the navigation visible (right).

This is what will make your responsive design actually act in a responsive manner. The device width will trigger your media queries and change the presentation of your site based on them.

To learn more about the meta viewport tag, visit www.quirksmode.org/mobile/metaviewport/.

Implementing Breakpoints

With responsive and adaptive design in mind, talking about media queries is generally geared toward the implementation and use of *breakpoints*.

Breakpoints are coupled with the `viewport` meta tag and allow styles to be applied in different ways for different screens.

Media queries have excellent browser support. The following is a list of browsers that have full support for media queries:

- IE9+
- IE Mobile 10+
- Firefox 3.5+

- Firefox for Android 26+

- Chrome 4+

- Chrome for Android 32+

- Safari 4.0+

- iOS Safari 3.2+

- Opera 9.5+

- Opera Mini 5.0+

- Opera Mobile 10.0+

- Android Browser 2.1+

- Blackberry Browser 7.0+

Using a Media Query

Getting started with media queries might seem technically confusing at first. This is not surprising—it does feel a little like technological alchemy. I find the best way to get started is to dive in and experiment. Take a look at the following sample media query:

```
@media screen and (min-width: 0px) and (max-width: 480px) {
  /* Styles go here*/
}
```

The media query sets up a breakpoint for screens that are between 0 and 480px wide. This is accomplished by setting up various conditions. The first is `screen`, which applies to any device with a screen. The second is `min-width: 0px,` and the third is `max-width: 480px`. When these conditions are all met, the code inside the braces is executed.

This can be determined by the media query starting with `@media screen`, which tells you that the following information will be applied to any device that reports having a screen. Next, you can see that two sections in parentheses contain values of `min-width` and `max-width`. Both of these properties have values entered that determine both the smallest screen and the largest screen that will be supported.

Note that the settings are strung together with the word `and`. This works like a run-on sentence, allowing multiple settings to be evaluated for the setup of the breakpoint.

Applying styles is then accomplished by adding styles inside the braces of the query. The following is the media query with some styles applied:

```
@media screen and (min-width: 0px) and (max-width: 480px) {
  body {font-family: helvetica, arial, sans-serif;font-size: 16px}
  h1 {color: #3333FF;font-size: 150%;}
  p {font-style: italic}
  a {color: #00CC00}
}
```

Figure 6.2 shows how these styles are rendered on a phone as well as a tablet.

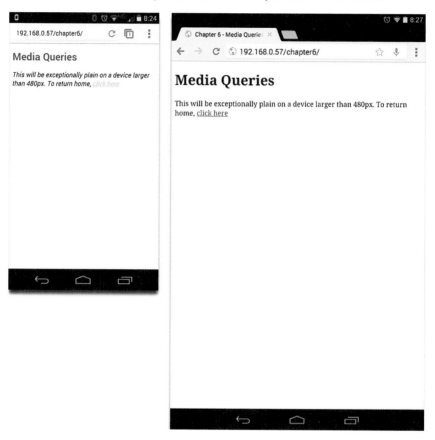

Figure 6.2   The phone (left) has a display that is between 0 and 480px, allowing styles (including the use of italic text) to be applied. The tablet (right) is wider than 480px and thus does not have styles applied.

As Figure 6.2 shows, the styles that were declared within the media query did not get applied to the tablet. This is because the tablet has a screen width of 600px, which is outside the 480px limit of the media query.

This is part of the reason using breakpoints is both fun and frustrating. There are a few different approaches to creating a CSS file in regard to this particular issue. The structure with which I have found the most success is to keep the mobile-first approach but put a slight spin on it.

First, I define the global styles. This includes element styles and utility or generic classes. Remember that anything in the "generic" section will be applied to all devices.

Next, I define my small screen breakpoint. This is usually for devices from 0 to 480px. This covers a majority of phones and other similar devices, such as portable media players.

The medium-sized screen is defined next. This varies depending on the project, but it generally covers screens from 481 to 959px wide. This size is one that you will need to fine-tune because it covers a very wide area; you might consider breaking this one in half to suit your needs.

The large media query is then defined at 960–1399px. This covers most large tablets that are in landscape orientation, as well as most laptops and desktop computers.

The extra-large-screened devices are then given a media query that covers anything above 1400px. This covers most high-resolution displays and television screens.

Listing 6.1 displays the contents of an example file with breakpoints set and ready for use.

Listing 6.1   Sample CSS File with Breakpoints Defined

```
body {
  font-family: "HelveticaNeue-Light", "Helvetica Neue Light", "Helvetica Neue",
Helvetica, Arial, "Lucida Grande", sans-serif;
  font-weight: 300;
}

/* Consider using intrinsic ratio instead of the following for image scaling */
img {
  max-width: 100%;
  vertical-align: bottom;
  height: auto;
  border: none;
}

/* Utility Classes */
.bold {font-weight: bold;}
.center {text-align: center;}

@media screen and (min-width: 0px) and (max-width: 479px) {
  /** Styles for 0-479 (small) screens **/
}

@media screen and (min-width: 480px) and (max-width: 959px) {
  /** Styles for 480-959 (mid) screens **/
}

@media screen and (min-width: 960px) and (max-width: 1399px) {
  /** Styles for 960-1399 (large) screens **/
}
```

```
@media screen and (min-width: 1400px) {
   /** Styles for 1400-infinity (xlarge) screens **/
}
```

Starting at the top of Listing 6.1, the global styles are applied to the `body` and `img` elements. The utility classes `.bold` and `.center` are then defined. These classes will be available to all screen sizes because they are not specifically defined within any of the media queries. Next in the file are sections that contain the breakpoints for various screen sizes. Inside each media query is a comment explaining what placing a style in that breakpoint will affect. Take note of the last media query: It does not contain a `max-width` property, but instead contains only the `min-width` property. This is because it covers any size screen above the minimum.

Figure 6.3 shows what would happen if you applied a style to the body element in each media query that changed the background across multiple devices.

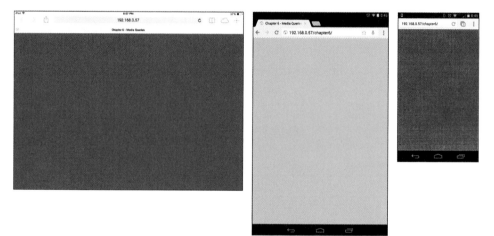

Figure 6.3   The background has changed colors for each screen size because of the styles contained in different media queries.

Another media query that you might find useful even though it isn't related to breakpoints is a section dedicated to pixel-dense screens. It enables you to load images for devices that have at least a ratio of 2.0 (such as Retina-display iPads and iPhones).

By adding the following snippet, you can place declarations for images that should be displayed on these high-resolution devices:

```
@media only screen and (-webkit-min-device-pixel-ratio: 2.0),
 only screen and (min-moz-device-pixel-ratio: 2.0),
 only screen and (min-device-pixel-ratio: 2.0) {
   /* styles for Retina displays go here */
}
```

This media query is a little different from the rest. It uses a different property as well. The `only` property makes older browsers (ones that are not likely to be found on high-pixel-density devices) ignore the media query. Also note that the conditions used in this query look different because they reference the actual device instead of the reported width of the viewport, like the conditions in previous snippets. If a device has a browser that is too old or does not meet any of the conditions, the style will not be rendered.

The query also contains some browser-prefixed code that allows WebKit-based browsers, such as Safari, and Mozilla-based browsers, such as Firefox, to read and apply the media query as the browser dictates.

The `min-device-pixel-ratio` property is used as the measurement to start applying these styles. This number is used as a comparative value between the styles to be applied and the actual pixel ratio of the device rendering the page.

The following is a snippet of CSS code that shows a background image being replaced for high-pixel-density devices:

```
.demo {
  background: transparent url(../images/bg_low.jpg) no-repeat;
  width: 320px;
  height: 100px;
}

@media only screen and (-webkit-min-device-pixel-ratio: 2.0),
only screen and (min--moz-device-pixel-ratio: 2.0),
only screen and (min-device-pixel-ratio: 2.0) {
  .demo {
    background: transparent url(../images/bg_high.jpg) no-repeat;
    width: 320px;
    height: 100px;
    background-size: 320px 100px;
  }
}
```

Note that image paths used in the snippet are relative to the project path. For your own project, you should be either using the absolute path or referencing the file with a fully qualified domain reference. Figure 6.4 shows the results of this media query on a device with a high pixel density, as well as on a device with a low pixel density.

Depending on the device demographics for your site, you might find it best to set specific media queries to handle devices instead of using conditions that span different viewport sizes or other device-related queries.

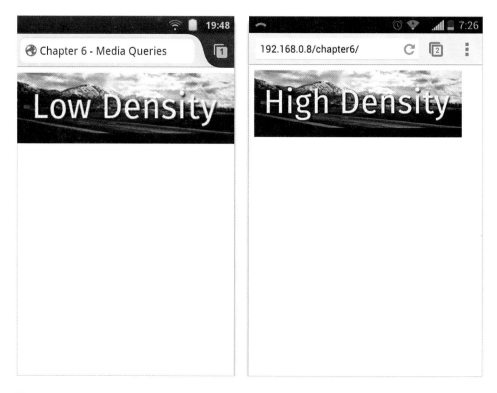

Figure 6.4   The image is rendered on a device with a low pixel ratio (left), as well as a device with a high pixel ratio (right). The image displayed changes based on the media query for pixel ratio.

IE6-8 Browser Support

You can leverage several polyfills that give support for your media queries. The one I find myself using the most is RespondJS (https://github.com/scottjehl/Respond), by Scott Jehl.

You can include this polyfill directly or conditionally after your CSS file includes. It gives users of IE6-8 support for your media queries. Note that not all media queries (such as nested media queries) are supported. For a full list of known issues, as well as implementation guidelines, view the instructions on the GitHub page.

Device-Specific Media Queries

Targeting specific devices can be frustrating, especially when you are trying to focus on a specific iPad but not all iPads. Sometimes targeting a specific device is necessary for a project. This can happen when creating enterprise projects for which all users will be using a specific tablet or phone. Instead of having to isolate these devices on the server and create different pages or sites for them, you can create the same site and then use media queries to tailor the site usage and appearance to the device.

Another example is when you want to create site buttons or navigation. Many Android users are accustomed to using the application drawer to access the options available to them. The same principle can be applied to iOS users, who are accustomed to having commonly used buttons at the bottom of the screen instead of the top.

Targeting specific devices is possible, but it requires knowing the target device's width and height, as well as the pixel ratio. Following are some media queries for popular devices.

> Tip
>
> When using device-specific media queries, the styles will not work on another device unless the screen size and pixel ratio (if included) match exactly. Test on as many actual devices as possible.

iPad

The iPad is an interesting device to target because only some of them include high-pixel-density displays.

There is good news about these differences, however: You can use a generic media query to target all iPads or add an option to check for the pixel ratio of the device to fine-tune your target.

To target the iPad 1, 2, and Mini (1st Generation):

```
@media screen
and (device-width: 768px)
and (device-height: 1024px) and (-webkit-device-pixel-ratio: 1) {
  /* add styles here*/
}
```

To target the iPad 3, 4, Air, and Mini (2nd Generation):

```
@media screen
and (device-width: 768px)
and (device-height: 1024px) and (-webkit-device-pixel-ratio: 2) {
/* add styles here*/
}
```

To target all iPads, you can remove the `and (-webkit-device-pixel-ratio: 1)` from the first snippet. This removes the condition for pixel density, so all iPads will use the styles contained within the media query.

iPhone Through 4S

You can target the iPhone 2, 3, and 4 with media queries aimed at a minimum width of 320px and a maximum width of 480. You can also throw in specific styles based on the orientation of the device by specifying a value as either `portrait` or `landscape`.

To target the iPhone regardless of screen orientation:

```
@media only screen and (min-device-width: 320px) and (max-device-width:
➡480px) {
  /* add styles here */
}
```

To target the iPhone in portrait orientation:

```
@media only screen
and (min-device-width: 320px)
and (max-device-width: 480px) and (orientation: portrait) {
  /* add styles here */
}
```

To target the iPhone in landscape orientation:

```
@media only screen
and (min-device-width: 320px)
and (max-device-width: 480px) and (orientation: landscape) {
  /* add styles here*/
}
```

iPhone 5 and 5S

The iPhone 5 and 5S have a taller screen than previous iPhone models, so they use a different media query. As with the media queries used on the other iPhones, you can set styles for the orientation of the device.

To target the iPhone 5 and 5S in both landscape and portrait orientation:

```
@media only screen and (min-device-width: 320px) and (max-device-width:
➡568px) {
  /* add styles here*/
}
```

To target the iPhone 5 and 5S in portrait orientation:

```
@media only screen
and (min-device-width: 320px)
and (max-device-width: 568px) and (orientation: portrait) {
  /* add styles here */
}
```

To target the iPhone 5 and 5S in landscape orientation:

```
@media only screen
and (min-device-width: 320px)
and (max-device-width: 568px) and (orientation: landscape) {
  /* add styles here */
}
```

Nexus 7 (2nd Generation)

The Nexus 7 is one of the most popular Android tablets available. The second generation improved on the first by increasing the resolution as well as the pixel ratio.

To target the Nexus 7 (2nd Generation) regardless of screen orientation:

```
@media screen and (device-width: 600px) and (device-height: 912px) {
  /* add styles here */
}
```

Note that using `device-width` and `device-height` tests the exact pixel values. This makes it highly unlikely that other devices will trigger this media query.

Galaxy S4

The Galaxy S4 has a unique screen resolution. It is billed as 1080x1920, but because of the pixel ratio, it actually renders at 320px wide and 640px tall when viewed in portrait orientation.

To target the Galaxy S4:

```
@media screen
and (device-width: 320px)
and (device-height: 640px) and (-webkit-device-pixel-ratio: 3) {
  /* add styles here */
}
```

Many devices exist, with thousands of various resolutions. As the designer or developer, it is always a good idea to test as often and as thoroughly as possible. Unless you need a very specific style, it is better to use ranges to cover the wide variety of resolutions available.

A couple excellent resources can help you determine the width and height of your device, as well as the pixel ratio. Visit http://mqtest.io and http://ryanve.com/lab/dimensions on your desktop, tablet, or mobile device for help with writing media queries for your site.

Summary

In this chapter, you learned about the origin of the media query and how you can use it to apply styles to specific devices. You also learned that it is compatible with most modern browsers, including mobile ones.

In addition, you learned about the `meta` tag and the role it plays in regard to media queries. Finally, you learned about using specific media queries to target specific devices.

CHAPTER 7

TYPOGRAPHY

Print designers have known for years that there's more to a design than choosing a color and adjusting masks and elements. A good design needs a hook that is subtle and informative and that conveys its playful, serious, mad, or even whimsical nature.

Typography helps bridge the gap between the sparkle and fade of our design. It helps draw users in and gives them an instant feel for the product or service. In mobile design, choosing the correct font can be critical for achieving success.

Web Fonts

As a designer, you are probably keenly aware that, more often than not, your dream font is not available on every device and every browser.

You likely gained this knowledge from the process of designing and developing a site yourself—or from a horrifying experience such as having your developer show you the implementation of your design and feeling part of you die while viewing your original font choice rendered down into an abomination that makes Comic Sans look vaguely desirable.

You might have even decided to give up the fight of using the perfect font for the entire site and opted to use it only on special portions of the design as an image.

This, you tell yourself, will help you sleep at night and fix all the problems in the world. Your users will surely see the effort you have put into product names, hero images, and various call-to-action buttons.

Unfortunately, because of the increased pixel ratio of devices, the regular text on your site now appears crisp and sharp, whereas your sacrificial "stylized" renderings now offer users no quarter, as they contend with blurred lettering, rough edges, and pixelation worthy of an 8-bit video game.

Do not despair, however: You do have an answer. For a few years, this scenario bordered on the nearly impossible, or even in the "works on every device and browser except the one you need it to work on" realm. But now you have a valid solution: the web font.

Web fonts come in different formats so that a browser can download and use them. They also come with a few compatibility cautions. To help you implement them correctly and guarantee that you are using quality fonts, several services are available.

Font Formats

Using fonts on the web is both similar and dissimilar to using fonts on your own computer. Your computer might be able to use TrueType, OpenType, and perhaps even PostScript fonts, but when it comes to the Web, the supported fonts depend heavily on the browser that is interpreting them.

The formats commonly used are TTF, EOT, WOFF, and SVG.

TTF

The TrueType (TTF) font format has existed since the 1980s and has enjoyed a rather long, popular life thanks to the support of Windows and Apple systems.

This format is compatible with almost every modern browser, leaving only Opera Mini and Internet Explorer (including IE Mobile) unable to use the format.

Also worth noting is that OpenType (OTF) files can be interchanged with TTF files and have the same browser support.

To see which browsers currently support TTF/OTF, visit http://caniuse.com/ttf.

EOT

Microsoft created Embedded OpenType (EOT) as a way to help distribute fonts through the Web. These fonts are created by starting with a TrueType font and then using a conversion process to create the EOT version of it.

This format was submitted as the official format for web fonts, but the W3C ultimately rejected it and replaced it with the WOFF format.

Because the EOT format is a Microsoft creation and was rejected as the standard for web fonts, it is compatible only with desktop versions of Internet Explorer. At the time of this writing, no versions of IE Mobile supported EOT.

WOFF

W3C members and developers decided that the Web Open Font Format (WOFF) would be the standard for deliverable web fonts.

As the agreed-upon standard for web font delivery, WOFF is supported by every major modern browser except Opera Mini.

Currently, version 1.0 of WOFF has been approved and considered a complete work in CSS3. A draft of WOFF version 2 was started in 2014. It contains suggestions such as sending both version 1 and 2 formats to increase browser support and including new compression algorithms and preprocessing data to reduce redundancy.

To see which browsers currently support WOFF, visit http://caniuse.com/woff.

SVG

The Scalable Vector Graphics (SVG) format is used extensively for icons and images that need to retain clarity without regard to pixel density.

Many agree that this particular format was meant not for use as a body font, but rather as a means to add flair and intrigue to an otherwise boring display.

Regarding mobile Safari, before iOS 4.2, the only way to use a web font was to use an SVG font. Today many browsers support SVG fonts, although Firefox has decided to focus on WOFF and has not added support for SVG fonts. Internet Explorer and Opera Mini do not support SVG fonts, either.

Browser and Device Support

I often hear the expression that "the devil is in the details." When dealing with the myriad devices available and browsers they run, this expression is quite accurate. The overall inclusion of web fonts isn't the problem—it's the smaller details of getting everything put together.

Depending on the software a device uses and the browser used, you can expect to see some different behavior.

Device Differences

You know that iOS and Android are operating systems, but did you know that they have some default system fonts? The following list shows some of the system fonts that are either included or used on each platform:

- **iOS:** Helvetica Neue
- **Android:** Droid Sans, Roboto
- **Firefox OS:** Fira Sans, Fira Monotype
- **Tizen:** Tizen Sans
- **Mobile Ubuntu:** Ubuntu, Ubuntu Monotype

> **Tip**
>
> A mobile OS might not be limited to one or two system fonts. For example, iOS shares many of the same fonts that OS X has. To see a list of the fonts available for iOS devices, visit http://support.apple.com/kb/HT5878.

A fun fact that you might not know is that, of the fonts just listed, all but Helvetica Neue are open source fonts that you can download and use. You have probably heard of "web safe fonts": These are fonts that are installed on many operating systems and can therefore be used "safely" on any system. As more mobile devices enter the market, this list of fonts that are safe to use changes. It is recommended that you use multiple fonts when declaring your font family so that the browser has a choice of fallback fonts. An example of this is Better Helvetica, by Chris Coyier (http://css-tricks.com/snippets/css/better-helvetica/). Feel free to mix and match your own fonts for your project.

Some browsers have an internal list of fonts to use if they cannot find a system font. This might not be a problem, but if you are counting on a serif font, you might be surprised when your page is suddenly rendered with a sans-serif font.

To illustrate how using a font family works, Figure 7.1 shows a page rendered on different operating systems. You can see how the fonts vary depending on what the device supports.

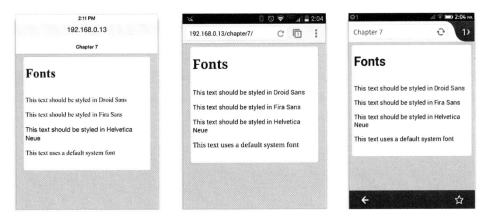

Figure 7.1   iOS (left), Android (middle), and Firefox OS (right) display fonts based on system rules.

As Figure 7.1 shows, each OS has displayed the text in a font that it supports. Android does not support Helvetica Neue or Fira Sans, so it has used a fallback font to display text. If you used a common web font, each device would show the same font.

As mentioned earlier, some browsers, such as the mobile version of Firefox (including the Android Firefox Browser), use a sans-serif font as the default font instead of the traditional serif font.

Figure 7.2 shows how the page is rendered on different devices when a web font is used.

Browser Behavior

Knowing that different devices might not support the font you would like to use, you also have to worry about browser support.

> **Tip**
>
> Opera Mini does not support `@font-face`. This shouldn't be too surprising: The browser is geared toward the feature phone market rather than the smartphone market.

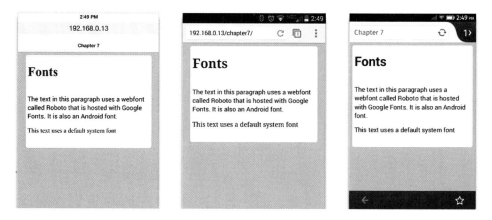

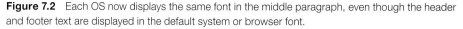

Figure 7.2 Each OS now displays the same font in the middle paragraph, even though the header and footer text are displayed in the default system or browser font.

As you learned earlier in the chapter, almost every modern browser supports web fonts. However, just because it is supported doesn't mean you should jump for joy and start throwing as many fonts as you want in your design.

The reason you shouldn't quickly abandon all your senses and plaster your site with multiple fonts (other than that it will end up looking like a ransom note) is that every web font has a hidden price. That price is data.

You could argue with yourself and rationalize that mobile users are at home on broadband speeds and not in a store or cafe or out with friends when they are looking at your site, so it doesn't need to be small. Of course, you'd be wrong, but you'd probably feel pretty good about it.

Paying close attention to which styles you are willing to use and how many files you will be downloading is crucial to mobile users, who might have to wait an extra 1–3 seconds for your fonts to load.

As an example, the OpenSans font is available in bold, bold italic, extra bold, extra bold italic, italic, light, light italic, regular, semibold, and semibold italic. That is 10 different styles for one font. If you sized these by the smallest version available (WOFF, in this case), you would add an extra 232KB to your page, along with 10 URL requests, for a potential 200–1000ms of load time per request.

Doing some quick math, by including every style of the OpenSans font, you could end up adding more than 10 seconds of load time to your page. For a mobile user, this is roughly the length of time it takes to order a pizza, post an update about your favorite show, and watch an entire season of *Game of Thrones*.

This might be an extreme example, and many fonts can have multiple styles added into one request. I mention this, however, because I have worked on projects for which more than 12 fonts were chosen for a single web project.

This is especially concerning for eCommerce sites. A study published in January 2014 (http://programming.oreilly.com/2014/01/web-performance-is-user-experience.html) found that, for every 160KB of images included on the Etsy site, the bounce rate of visitors increased by 12%. That study might have called out the bounce rate for images, but think of this in terms of typography directly related to style and presentation: If the page will not load because it is waiting to download styles, a user is still going to get frustrated and leave.

> ## Tip
>
> Many resources are available for testing the speed of your site. Some are more involved than others, but be sure to visit the following for information and tools to monitor and improve the speed of your site:
>
> - PageSpeed Insights (http://developers.google.com/speed/pagespeed/insights/)
> - GTmetrix (http://gtmetrix.com/)
> - Pingdom Tools (http://tools.pingdom.com/fpt/)
> - Sitespeed.io (www.sitespeed.io/)
> - WebPageTest (www.webpagetest.org/)
> - SpeedCurve (http://speedcurve.com/http://speedcurve.com/)
> - Torbit (http://torbit.com/)

The solution for this is to limit the number of font resources you use. If you can get by with including the regular style and the bold or heavy style of the font, do so; skip the multiple fonts or styles that are used only once.

Another important reason to minimize the use of multiple web fonts is that if you use a font that includes complex glyphs (which increase the size of the font file) and you specify that font for copy on your site, users might experience a site that does not contain any text. This is because the text will not be rendered until the font has been downloaded and initialized.

To avoid this issue, specify a fallback font or two on the body element and then apply your specialty font by using a class. This might cause the page to "flicker" or suddenly change because the text will load with one font and then suddenly change when the web font has been downloaded. Unless your design absolutely hinges on the web font being there when the user views the page, consider this a means to deliver content to the user.

Serving Web Fonts

When you settle on the font you want to use and have decided on the format(s) it will be distributed in, you need to use CSS to tell the browser how to use the font.

The CSS rule used to include custom fonts is `@font-face`. This rule enables you to specify the font(s) you would like to include in your site. The following is a sample of including the Regular font from the OpenSans family:

```
@font-face {
  font-family: 'open_sansregular';
  src: url('OpenSans-Regular-webfont.eot');
  src: url('OpenSans-Regular-webfont.eot?#iefix')
➡format('embedded-opentype'),
       url('OpenSans-Regular-webfont.woff') format('woff'),
       url('OpenSans-Regular-webfont.ttf') format('truetype'),
       url('OpenSans-Regular-webfont.svg#open_sansregular')
➡format('svg');
  font-weight: normal;
  font-style: normal;
}
```

To get technical on what is happening with this CSS snippet, the rule of `@font-face` is created and wraps the `font-family`, `src`, `font-weight`, and `font-style` properties. The `src` properties all point to where the file lives in relation to the CSS file (because no path is specified in this example, the font files are in the same folder or directory as the CSS file). The `font-weight` and `font-style` are used to set the default values for the font and can be changed according to your unique tastes.

Now that the font has been set up, you need to either create a class that uses the font or add the font to an existing element. The following shows how you can apply the font by using a CSS class:. `open-sans {font-family: 'open_sansregular';}`

Here, the class `open-sans` can now be applied to different elements and will style them with the OpenSans Regular font. Figure 7.3 shows a paragraph styled with the font and another paragraph using the default font styles.

> ### Tip
>
> When hosting your own custom fonts, some web servers need to be told how to serve the files so that browsers will understand what the files are. If you are using Apache, locate your `httpd.conf` file and add the following:
>
> ```
> AddType application/vnd.ms-fontobject .eot
> AddType application/x-font-opentype .otf
> AddType image/svg+xml .svg
> AddType application/x-font-ttf .ttf
> AddType application/font-woff .woff
> ```

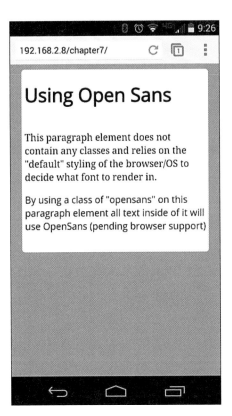

Figure 7.3   The top paragraph does not have the custom font applied, but the lower paragraph does.

Using Font Services

The benefit of using a hosted font service is that these services use content delivery networks to distribute requested font files from servers that are closer and, in theory, faster than your web server. Another benefit is that, if the user has loaded a font from a provider, it might still be cached in the browser, so your page will render with the font you want without making the user wait for it to download and then display.

Google Fonts

Google offers a service for web fonts and currently has a collection of more than 600 fonts, including serif, sans-serif, display, handwriting, and monospace-styled fonts.

Visit www.google.com/fonts to browse and search the font directory and add styles you like to a collection. After you create a collection, you can review how the collection will look with sample titles, paragraphs, or custom text. You can then fine-tune how many styles of each font you would like to include in your font request and see the impact on page load.

> ## Tip
>
> If you are using a Google Font but only for a handful of characters, you can make a request for a font and limit the glyphs sent. This reduces file size and increases the speed of your page rendering. To achieve this, add a parameter of `text=` to the `link` element and specify the characters you want. A sample request looks like the following:
>
> ```
> <link href='http://fonts.googleapis.com/css?family=Duru+Sans&text=
> ➥SpecialTxt'rel='stylesheet' type='text/css'>
> ```

Adobe Typekit

Adobe has been in the font game from the beginning. To continue its tradition of font perfection, Adobe has acquired and maintains the font service named Typekit.

Typekit (originally created by Small Batch and acquired by Adobe in 2011) aims to be the one service that works cross-platform and cross-browser to help designers achieve the exact design they have in mind while overcoming the obstacles of manually managing fonts and working to redeploy the code that runs your site.

Because this is a premium service, several plans are available. The free plan is good for users who have less than 25,000 page views a month and is limited to two fonts. If you are just getting started with a font service, this is a great place to start.

Paid plans are rather affordable, ranging from $24 to $99 a month, with increased usage limits and number of sites the fonts can be used on.

Visit https://typekit.com/ to learn more.

Fonts.com

Similar to Typekit, Fonts.com offers more than 150,000 different fonts that you can incorporate and use on your site. This service offers plans that let you host the fonts yourself, download and use them on your computer, and use its CDN to serve files to users. It also offers an analytics package to help track users and manage your font usage.

Other services, such as for hosting branded fonts, are available and might be of interest to business and enterprise users who work with outside parties and do not want to worry about file distribution.

Similar to Typekit, they allow you to pick fonts for each project or site and then publish changes without having to change much of your site code.

They have plans ranging from free to $100 a month. Most allow users to sign up and try the service before committing to a long-term service agreement.

Font Squirrel

If you are looking for an alternative font provider that offers many royalty-free commercial-use fonts, Font Squirrel might be your best option.

Font Squirrel offers fonts for desktop, application, web fonts, and more. You can filter by type and even browse a list of curated "almost free" fonts for use.

One of the best features, however, is the web font generator (www.fontsquirrel.com/tools/webfont-generator). It allows you to upload a font from your computer and then gives you fine-tuned control over how to create fonts suitable for web distribution.

Note that Font Squirrel does maintain a blacklist of fonts that are of restricted license and will not allow you to make web fonts out of them.

Icon Fonts

Another consideration when using fonts is using an icon font. Recently, many developers have been moving toward using SVG files for icons and applying SVG filters to them for desired effects and animation.

The method of using SVG files for icons is a great idea for browsers that support SVG filters and animation, but that support is currently limited. Instead, you can use a font that contains glyphs of icons and logos. By then including this font on your site, you can apply any CSS that you would apply to standard text; you also get icons that scale with text of your site.

This means that color, drop shadow, layering, sizing with em units, and more is all available for the icons of your site. It also means that you do not have to worry about including @2x icons that would be used on high-pixel-density devices.

You should be aware, however, that icon fonts have some potential pitfalls. Icon fonts are generally limited to a single color. This might not be a bad thing, but your font also might clash with the rest of your design. Icon fonts can also run into the problem of having glyphs included in the reserved section of a font. This can render fine on your local machine thanks to your text encoding, but users from other locales might see boxes, question marks, or even giant X symbols where your icon should be.

The easiest way to use an icon font is to head over to IcoMoon (http://icomoon.io/). From there, you can sign up for services and have your custom icon fonts created and served, or you can use the IcoMoon app. The app is a tool that enables you to choose from a variety of icons that can be placed into a font, with generated PNG files that you can use as a fallback solution for devices that do not support icon fonts.

Summary

In this chapter, you learned how to use a specialized font on the Web. You learned the methods you can leverage to make sure all devices will be able to load your font, and you explored the browsers that support various formats of web fonts.

You looked into services that you can leverage to help serve and distribute your font.

You also discovered that some solutions, such as icon fonts, can display logos and icons in a way that many browsers support. And you found out about the IcoMoon service, which offers a fallback solution by using PNG files.

CHAPTER 8

RETROFITTING AN EXISTING SITE

It doesn't matter whether you are working for yourself, as a freelancer, for a corporation, or even as part of a design studio—at some point, you will be asked to take an existing site and make it work on everything.

This might seem overwhelming but is by no means impossible. In this chapter, you learn about choosing the proper layout, working with site components, and keeping some important issues in mind when going mobile.

When starting the conversion process, I work through three basic areas. I start by creating a block-level layout of my current design, then I work on handling each component, and finally, I work on adding and fine-tuning features to make the mobile experience more enjoyable, easy to use, and more native.

You will need to determine your layout while you work through the existing design. A responsive design layout gives you a fluid and flexible site, whereas an adaptive approach helps you ease into the fluid process by giving you some elements of pixel-perfect layouts while exposing your design to media query–based control. You might also end up with a hybrid layout that uses elements of both responsive and adaptive design.

Choosing a Proper Layout for Mobile

Most sites that are in need of conversion to mobile devices have been designed to fit somewhere between 960px and 1140px in width. With the iPhone 5 currently having a maximum visible resolution of 320x568px when viewed in portrait orientation and 568x320px when viewed in landscape orientation, you need to make many decisions and choices. Note also that these dimensions are the ones visible by dividing the actual number of pixels by the pixel density ratio (Retina screens have a ratio of 2, so 640x1136 becomes 320x568).

Block-Level Layout

You have many ways to begin the process of creating a design: You can break out the sketchbook and pencil, the prototype stencils, or any number of drag-and-drop applications. However, the method I lean on when working on retrofitting is the standard block-level layout.

If you are unfamiliar with block-level layout, the easiest thing to do is to look for the seams in your site. As a starting point to help you identify the blocks, you can use the following list:

- Header
- Side navigation or bar
- Content area
- Footer

To see this in action, Figure 8.1 shows a site with an overlay of how I would break down a site into blocks.

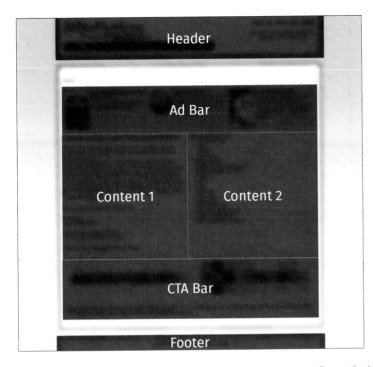

Figure 8.1   By grouping the site into content blocks, you can easily see the important areas of your site.

> **Tip**
>
> It can be difficult to take pictures of a currently rendered site, but you can make use of several applications. On OS X, try using the Paparazzi! application (http://derailer.org/paparazzi/) to easily save images of entire site pages. As a bonus, Paparazzi includes Automator scripts that you can leverage to automate your workflow.
>
> Windows users can use FireShot (http://getfireshot.com/) as a browser extension to capture site pages.

With the page broken down into blocks, you can get an idea of the content that each block contains, including components such as search areas, navigation, and widgets. This is helpful because it enables you to work on breaking down the site into smaller pieces and rearranging content to fit. Figure 8.2 demonstrates how the blocks are changed to show the page arranged to fit on a smaller screen.

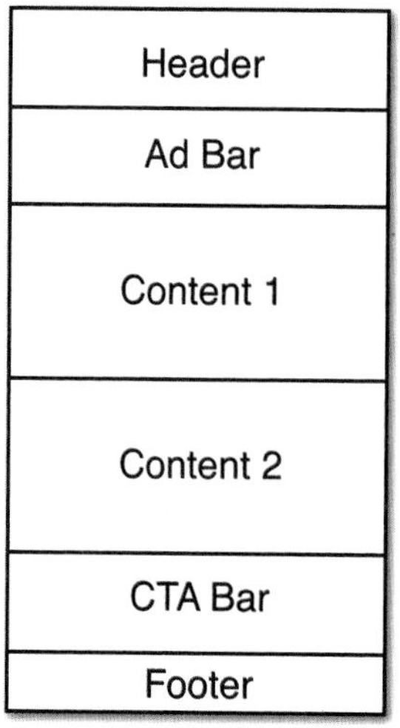

Figure 8.2   By rearranging the content blocks, you can visually see how the site will adapt for different screens. Note that some areas might change in size.

Even though all sections are visible, not all of them are actual size. You will need to change them based on the amount of content you have and how you decide to present them. It is also important to note that you will still need to work with the "fold." Mobile devices can make dealing with the fold complicated because you will have no way to reliably handle where the fold is exactly. If you have an analytics page on your site (Google Analytics, Adobe Omniture, or similar service), you should be able to get a list of device resolutions and construct a suitable landing experience for most of your users.

You can use various methods to create your layout. You can even get creative with bits of paper by cutting them out at the size you want and writing the name of the component in them. The point of using the block-level layout is to see how the page is going to flow and react based on the screen of the device viewing your site.

Now that you have a rough layout, it is time to decide whether you will be embracing a responsive layout or an adaptive one.

Responsive Layout

You know that using a responsive layout means that everything needs to be fluid and flowing and that it will use as much available space as it can get its pixel-loving virtual hands on.

This type of layout has little to no waste of screen real estate, but it also generally has enough whitespace to calm the mind and keep users from feeling forced into a cave so that they start breathing into a paper bag before claustrophobia sets in and they ultimately smash the Close Tab button on their browser and head for open spaces.

Choosing to roll with a responsive layout means that you now need to think about the following:

- Flexible percentage or em-based layout, with gutters that change based on screen width
- Text that might break in odd places
- Images that need to be swapped out or allowed to scale
- Acceptance of a design that is no longer pixel perfect

> **Tip**
>
> An em unit is the equivalent of the base unit of measurement on the body of your page. The general default is 16px. This can be helpful in doing quick layout changes without worrying about actual pixel values.

Figure 8.3 demonstrates how a site could transition from a small screen up to a larger one.

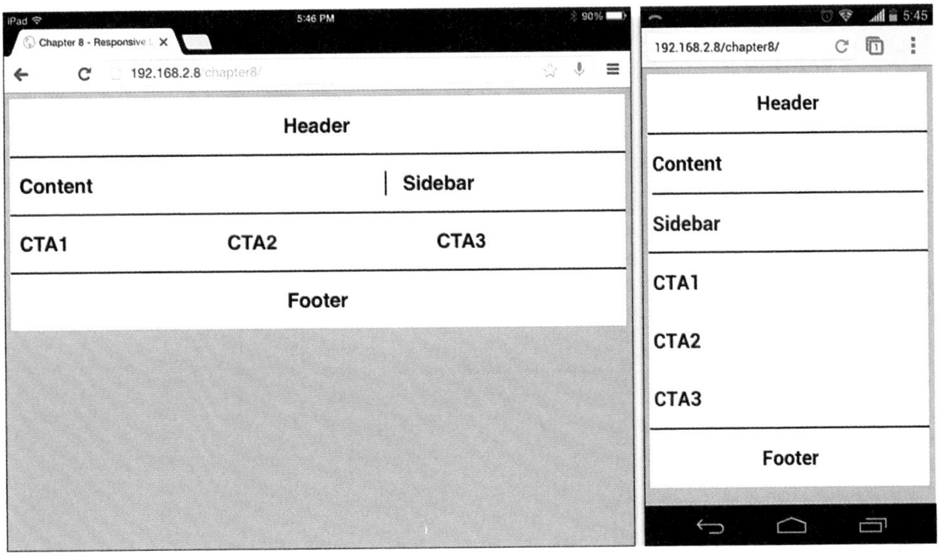

Figure 8.3   The content and image areas remain edge to edge as the transition is made to larger screens.

Embracing a fully responsive solution is difficult and requires serious planning and dedication for the design, user experience, and user interaction teams. Note that, in this design, CTA means *call to action*. These are areas of the design that draw users into clicking or tapping to see more information or lead them to a specific section of the site.

Adaptive Layout

Approaching your design with an adaptive layout can help others get used to the idea of using a design that changes depending on screen size and also gives some control back to your design. This is because of the locked-width flow of adaptive web design.

Whereas a responsive layout is a maximized experience, an adaptive layout gives you the capability to be pixel perfect. With each breakpoint, you set a maximum width for your content area and then use margins that grow until the next breakpoint is matched.

Figure 8.4 demonstrates how an adaptive layout transitions between sizes.

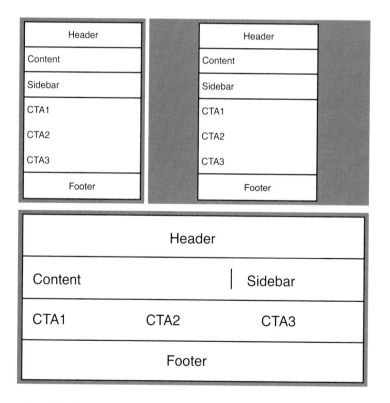

Figure 8.4 The design starts edge to edge (top left), but margins grow as the screen viewing the site increases in size (top right) until the next breakpoint is reached and the process starts over (bottom).

If you are a pixel-perfect designer, this method might work best because it will be more compatible with your existing flow and will feel like you are building mock-ups of the same site in different sizes.

No matter what layout you decide to use, you need to determine a method for handling all the components that are contained in each of the blocks of your site.

Working with Components

Everything in your site can be broken down into components. Sometimes these are simply elements. Other times, they are groups of elements. A search input, a navigation menu, and sliders are all examples of elements.

When creating the mobile or smaller versions of your site, you need to take into consideration what should happen to each of these elements.

Navigation

No matter how brilliant your current navigation system is, odds are, you will need to change it to make it fit on smaller devices.

You could always wrap the navigation to a new line; however, this often looks sloppy and comes across as lazy. Still, this will work if your navigation is text based and if you can align the words so that they are balanced and the line looks intentional instead of heavy on one side. If your navigation is reliant on hover states or mega menus, you will need to create a new system or method for handling all your links.

You should consider two other methods when you are compressing your navigation. The first is to use a menu that drops in, and the second is to use an off-canvas solution.

Both solutions require the use of a menu button or icon that will take the place of your text.

> ### Tip
>
> You might be thinking of immediately jumping on the "hamburger" icon for your menu. This might work for you, but consider a study that tested the hamburger icon, the word *Menu*, and the word *Menu* with a round border that made it look like a button (http://exisweb.net/mobile-menu-abtest). The results found that more users engaged with the word *Menu* when it appeared to be a button than with the other methods.

Applying a menu that will drop in requires either using multiple layers, injecting a block of code on a click or tap event, or using classes to change the height and visibility of the content area.

Using an off-screen navigation solution is similar, but it slides in the menu by using animation (either JavaScript or CSS3 transitions) to make the content appear. This should be familiar to you because it is the type of solution Facebook implements in its mobile application and is also used in many Google products as a way to access the menu. Google+ and Google Music use this type of navigation to give you access to settings, playlists, images, groups, and more.

Because every project is different, you will need to play with the breakpoints for when your site navigation changes from text to the menu change. Figure 8.5 demonstrates a site displayed at different sizes, with the navigation changing.

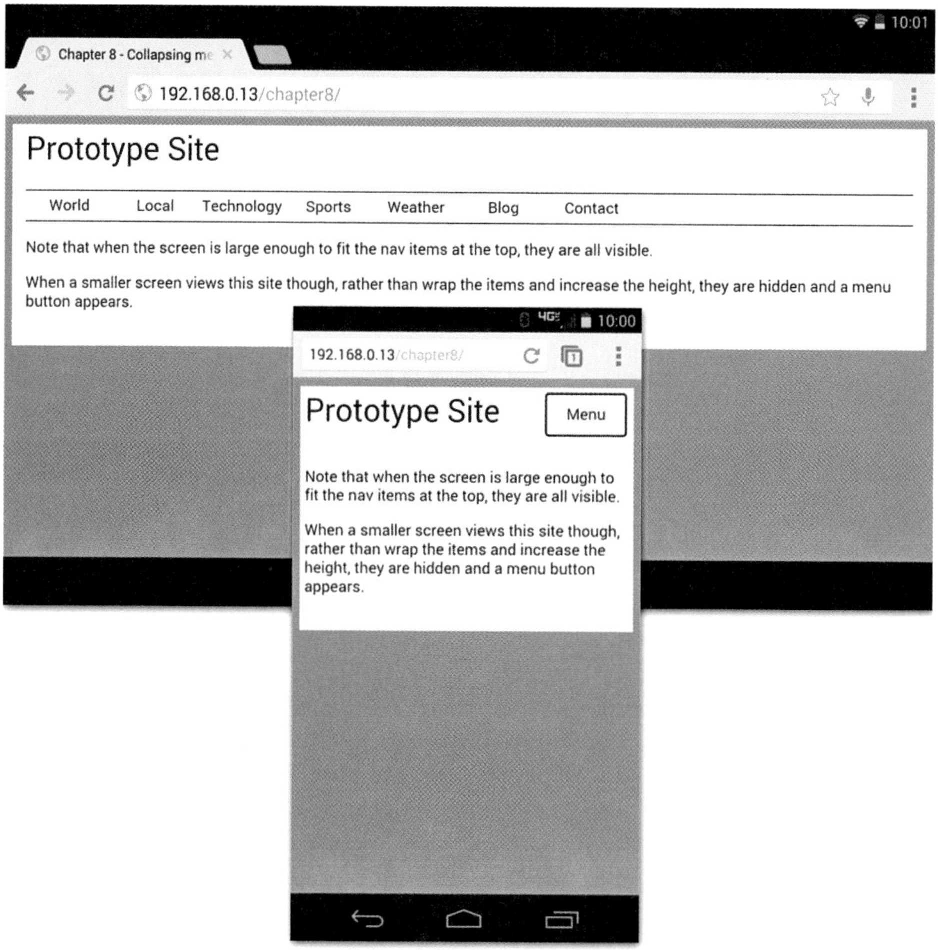

Figure 8.5   As the site is viewed on smaller devices, the navigation changes so that it is hidden until activated by the Menu button.

Some plugins might help you with your off-canvas navigation:

- Foundation Zurb (http://foundation.zurb.com/docs/components/offcanvas.html)
- Twitter Bootstrap (http://getbootstrap.com/examples/offcanvas/)
- Pushy (www.christopheryee.ca/pushy/)

Search

Unless your site has an absolute absence of content, you probably have a search box. The good news is that this particular search input adapts very well to mobile layouts.

Depending on your developers, there is already a fantastic chance that you are using the proper input element. HTML5 introduced a special `input` element made just for searching. It looks like the following:

```
<input type="search" name="search" />
```

The benefit of using the search input for your search is that mobile browsers can change the keyboard that appears to use it, and they can even add an icon and show you previous search entries when the field is activated.

The drawback of using this input is that some browsers automatically style the input to match the styles of the OS. For example, iOS rounds the corners of the input to make it appear like the default search element of iOS. This is good because the user can visually understand that it is a search field, but it is also bad because it could throw off your design (rounded corners on a flat design or a second magnifying glass added to the one you have already put on the page).

You have several options for handling the display of your search bar. You can choose to put it just below the header (which contains your logo and menu buttons) of your site, or you can choose to place it in the drop-in or off-canvas navigation area.

Either option is fine, but you should do some A/B testing, use heat maps, or apply other testing methods to make sure the search remains accessible and easy to find. Mobile users can be a finicky lot and will leave your site if they can't find what they need as fast as possible.

Content Areas

You might not give much thought to the content of your site, but if you are running a comparison site, an eCommerce site, or an informational site, you will run into the problem of having tons of content and not enough screen to properly display it all.

You have three common solutions for handling this particular issue:

- An **accordion** (or drawer) shows a particular title or question. The content is hidden until the title is tapped or clicked, when the accordion opens and shows the hidden content. This is commonly used on FAQ pages and pages that want to hide content-rich areas until the user has activated them.

  Note that some accordions allow only one section open at a time and automatically close any other open sections. Pay close attention to your user testing to make sure you are not frustrating users who would like to have multiple sections open at the same time.

- **Tab systems** are useful to display short terms that then open content areas that the user can then go through and view. This particular system suffers from the same autoclosing feature of some accordions and also forces you to cram buttons and text into a small space. This system works best on medium-size screens, but you can also use it successfully on smaller screens if you pay proper attention to text or icon size to activate the tabs.

- With a **grid system**, you have the option of arranging your content into columns. As the screen size of the device viewing your site shrinks, these columns will start to compress until you decide that the content is no longer legible. At this point, you can "break" the columns so that they take up 100% of the available width instead of the preassigned 25%, 33%, or 50% of screen space.

  The downside to using columns to break apart displayed content is that your pages have the potential to get very long. I'm not talking about a couple hundred pixels long—more like a carpel tunnel–inducing, finger-sprinting marathon of a page of long swipes. You should stick to using this particular style of content display for smaller content areas.

Sliders

I'll skip the discourse on sliders because I know that, when it comes down to it, some people will tell you that they absolutely need one. In addition, when you are working on retrofitting a site, you will need to know how to handle them.

First, because speed should be one of your primary objectives, you need to remember that sliders are inherently slow. This is the result of having to load multiple images into an area and then get them restyled so that they can be displayed in order. DOM processing is also slowed, and mobile devices will have to work harder to download, inject, and then redraw all the images on and off canvas as needed. Another side effect that you might not be aware of is the tradeoff in battery life. As the mobile device works harder to display your page, CPU and memory are used more and battery life can be affected.

Second, sliders are problematic on mobile devices because of the "pause on hover" effect that no longer works with mobile design. With this effect, the slider on a desktop would normally continue to show one slide after the other, but it stops when the mouse cursor is hovering or stopped on one of the slides. Mobile users might also become frustrated with sliders when they do not respond to screen swipes and when the users have no way of pausing or stopping the sliders.

Many mobile users are comfortable with the concept of swiping to move content around, but when that behavior is unavailable or seems to act funny due to slide timing, this can be a source of aggravation.

To successfully use a slider on mobile devices, remember the following:

- Let users move the slider.
- Make your slider touch/swipe friendly.
- Minimize the amount of data or number of slides in the slider.
- Load content by use of a deferred method (such as lazy loading) so that the site does not appear broken or waiting to load content.

A couple sliders that work well with mobile devices are BXSlider (http://bxslider.com/) and Owl Carousel (http://owlgraphic.com/owlcarousel/).

Links

A major consideration when moving from a desktop-only site is the size of your links. You might have noticed while visiting various sites that buttons and links are much larger when viewed on mobile devices. This goes deeper than just the Web: The developer guidelines for Windows Phone, Android, and iOS also specify that touch targets, or areas where the user can tap, should be big enough for a finger to tap.

How big is that, exactly? Well, it varies, and various pixel density values can make it somewhat difficult to narrow down. However, the following sizing values will get you started in the right direction:

- Use a minimum size of 34px by 34px, but consider using at least 44px.
- The width of your target can be longer than 44px, but the height should be at least 34px.
- Be sure to provide adequate space between targets—use at least 8px, to minimize accidental tapping.

Learn more about designing for touch devices by visiting these sites:

- iOS guidelines on Layout (https://developer.apple.com/library/ios/documentation/ UserExperience/Conceptual/MobileHIG/LayoutandAppearance.html#//apple_ref/doc/ uid/TP40006556-CH54-SW1)

- Windows Phone 8 Human Interface Guidelines (http://msdn.microsoft.com/en-us/library/windowsphone/develop/ff967556(v=vs.105).aspx)
- Android Metrics and Grids (http://developer.android.com/design/style/metrics-grids.html)

Considerations When Going Mobile

Knowing how to handle layout and some of the components will help in the retrofitting process, but you need to be aware of some other surprises.

For example, using the `:hover` CSS pseudo class is generally not a good idea with mobile devices. Having a click-to-call button, dealing with modal windows, and even using input fields are all extra matters that need to be taken into consideration.

No More Hover

Mobile devices are currently in an interesting place. Some devices, such as certain Samsung devices, can actually detect hovering fingers or stylus pens, but most devices cannot. Many laptop manufacturers have also started to include touchscreens, making this a potentially larger problem for more than just mobile devices.

This has a tendency to "break" the `:hover` CSS pseudo class. What happens is that you tend to get a tap-to-activate action that triggers the hover and then forces you to tap again to make your selection or dismiss the hover. This can get confusing and frustrating, depending on the touch target areas of your site. This doesn't mean that you can no longer use hover, but it requires you to think ahead.

Think about it this way: Let's say that you have a category with several items underneath that appear in a drop-down list that is triggered by using `:hover`. Now, if you had clicked on the category name to go to the category page, all your mobile visitors would have to tap the name once to activate the drop-down and then tap the name again to go to the category page.

This leaves the mobile user wondering whether tapping the category name will close the drop-down or take them somewhere. To get around this, you need to add a link named View All or similar so that mobile users know that they have a safe place to tap to get where they want to go.

Click to Call

People love convenience, and mobile users thrive on it. This might be the reason you need to consider adding a Click to Call button. This is not new: Maximiliano Firtman talked about doing this in 2010 (www.mobilexweb.com/blog/click-to-call-links-mobile-browsers). It seems that many designers and developers overlooked it.

You are likely aware of the major benefit of talking to a person when making a purchase. By adding a Click to Call element to your design, you empower your users and your marketing teams to help make both parties happy.

A simple way to add Click to Call to your site is with an anchor element, like the following:

```
<a href="tel:+15555555555"></a>
```

You want to make sure that you have styled the element to `display: block` and have added `width` and `height` values to it as well. Finally, you should consider adding an icon to it to help visually convey to users that, by tapping the icon, they can instantly dial the number. Also, for users not on a smartphone, this will appear as a link that does nothing. Some operating systems are looking to solve this issue by incorporating features that, when clicked from a desktop, will dial through various Voice Over IP systems or even push the call directly to your phone.

Modal Windows

Not long after everyone agreed that pop-up windows were a terrible idea because of potential distraction and mistrust (thanks to malware and infested sites that added Close buttons that actually installed malware instead of closing the window), the modal window was born. This particular style of window allowed pages, images, videos, and more to be displayed within the main window.

Many different types of modal windows are available, but they all have one thing in common: They are terribly implemented on mobile devices. What worked on your desktop design is suddenly not an option on mobile.

To design around this particular problem, you can use the following solutions: using a new window modal and using a resizing modal.

New Window Modal

Use a modal that takes users to a new page. This is similar to the approach that would be used with a framework such as jQuery Mobile. The modal window becomes a transition that displays a new page with a Close or Back button that takes users back to the original page.

The disadvantage of this particular style is that you are jarring the user with two experiences, and some users might not realize that they are on a new page that they need to close to get back to where they were.

This is of particular note when using product image galleries because moving users to a new page could cause them to become distracted or irritated that they left the page they wanted.

Resizing Modal

Many modal solutions currently employ a resizing technique to keep the contents of the window inside the available viewing space. These techniques work well for images (because most smartphone browsers can resize them to fit), but text content can be a major concern.

To handle the text elements, you need to either keep your content minimal or stick with using images. Regardless of the content, you need to make sure that close links are visible at all times so that users can exit the modal and return to the page they were on.

> ### Tip
>
> Test on the devices your users use. Unbelievable as it may seem, I created a modal window that worked perfectly for my devices (all had a minimum width of 360px), but I failed to test on an iPhone. My Close button was just barely offscreen and forced users to use the Back or Reload buttons on their browsers to get back to the page. This was a very costly mistake on my part. Don't learn this the hard way.

To visualize how a resizing modal works on multiple devices, see Figure 8.6, which shows the modal being used on an iPad and an Android phone.

Input Fields

The last consideration that needs your attention is the way your input forms work. You already know that search fields will change based on the input type; however, you might not have thought about how some of the built-in device features can sabotage your site.

You can leverage several HTML5 input types with properties to help get around these issues.

For email fields, use a type of `email` to add built-in browser validation:

```
<input type="email" name="email" />
```

Any iOS devices running iOS 5.0+ (which should be 100%) will, by default, disable the autocapitalization and autocorrect on this field. If you find that some users are still getting autocorrect or autocapitalization, you can add properties to the input like so:

```
<input type="email" name="email" autocorrect="off"
autocapitalize="off" spellcheck="false" />
```

This tells the browser that the field should not correct what the user has typed in. Note that these properties can also be used on text areas and text input elements.

It might seem like a small issue, and it doesn't play a direct role in the visual design process; however, as part of the user experience, paying attention to tiny interaction points is vital to a winning design, especially when it comes to mobile devices.

Figure 8.6 The image is clearly visible on both devices, while allowing access to close it.

Summary

In this chapter, you learned about the process of retrofitting a website. You learned about using a block-level strategy to isolate pieces of the site to work with, and then you moved on to working with the components that make up those blocks.

You also learned about many issues you need to be aware of when working a design to fit the needs of mobile users, including using sliders, hover states, search fields, text input fields, and modal windows.

PART II

WORKING WITH RESPONSIVE MEDIA

CHAPTER 9

RESPONSIVE IMAGES

Designs will always be epic, iconic, and awe inspiring. However, when thinking about the medium that users will be viewing your design on, it might be best to save some of that awe for the details and content delivery speed.

Using images that work on a variety of devices can be challenging. Luckily, you can start using some techniques and solutions to take your design into the future.

Images Should Be Responsive

It used to be that the most difficult part of exporting an image was deciding whether it worked better as a JPEG or GIF file. Those were simple days when it usually came down to determining the number of colors used and deciding whether transparency was important to me.

Then came PNG files, the solution that delivered the grandeur and scope of JPEG files and also gave images crisp and pristine transparency. It was definitely a step up, and many designers and developers still rely heavily on using PNG files. However, the file size for large images still leaves something to be desired. PNG files offer the same number of colors as JPEG files, but the file size ends up being far greater than with JPEG files because of the lossless compression that PNG uses in many image-manipulation programs. You might be able to save space by switching to a lossy PNG file, but JPEG files will almost always be smaller when used on complex, high-color images. As designers and developers, we are now dealing with incorporating SVG files and WEBP files.

All of these image formats are fantastic in their own respects, but the problem is dealing with them when they are too big or too small for the screen requesting them.

To give you an understanding of why images need to be responsive, in this chapter, you learn about delivering images to the browser by means of scaling, using new image elements, and using JavaScript to serve the correct image.

Delivering Images

When you are dealing with mobile devices, the images that you choose to use are extremely important. Detail, clarity, and even the emotion you are attempting to evoke can be dramatically shifted when your image is squished or broken on the page.

To give you a feel for what I am talking about, see Figure 9.1.

In Figure 9.1, you can easily see both the climber in the middle and the crowd below. If you viewed this same image on a phone, the scene either would be zoomed in or would have to scale to fit, as in Figure 9.2.

The image has been scaled so that everything is still visible, but this leaves less initial detail, especially on the climber, and might actually cause more visual confusion than would a different image.

Figure 9.1   The image is viewed on a desktop with everything in good detail.

Figure 9.2   When viewed on a phone, the scene is scaled to fit, making the subject more difficult to view.

Leaving the visuals aside, what does this do for users who are attempting to download the images? Well, for starters, it slows them down. The original image used for Figures 9.1 and 9.2 is a JPG that comes out at 344KB. That certainly doesn't sound like much, but when your site has 10 images of a similar size, you would be adding more than 3MB in images alone to what users have to download on their mobile devices, along with any JavaScript files and other data to view your site.

> ## Note
>
> 3MB of data doesn't sound very large when you have a fast broadband connection. However, that same 3MB of data can take up some time (as well as data) on wireless plans. The following lists the time to download a 3MB image:
>
> - 3G (1–4Mbps): 5–23 seconds
> - LTE (5–10Mbps): 2–4 seconds
> - DSL (1.5Mbps): 15 seconds
>
> Note that, even after downloading the image, the device still has to process and display the image. If you have multiple images, the time taken to load images will add up quickly.

If you were able to serve a different image based on device size, this would not only save in file size, but it would also enable you to choose the art direction of the image. Figure 9.3 shows the image optimized for mobile users.

Being able to choose exactly what is shown is helpful, and because this enables you to use a smaller image (this one is 49KB), you can be assured that the user will be able to download and view the image much faster.

While on the subject of the file size of your images, it might be worth using the WEBP image format on your site. This format has a wide array of features and uses a different compression algorithm, enabling you to save anywhere from 7% to 50% of original picture size. Figure 9.4 shows WEBP and JPEG images.

You have a few methods that you can employ to do what we have done here. In the next sections, you learn first about image scaling, then about using the `srcset` attribute, and then about using the `picture` element.

Figure 9.3 The visible portion of the image has changed for an optimal viewing experience on a mobile device.

Figure 9.4 Using WEBP, the top image is 56KB; the JPG image on the bottom is 111KB.

Image Scaling

One of the most common—and also most misunderstood—"responsive" image techniques is the use of image scaling via the browser. This doesn't involve any new images; it just requires a few lines of CSS. Applying the following in your CSS magically makes your images shrink to fit:

```
img {
  max-width: 100%;
  height: auto;
}
```

Note that IE8 users will notice a spectacular amount of fail with this example; to fix it, you should apply `width: 100%` before `max-width: 100%`. You should also be aware that, by setting an image to have a width of 100%, the image might attempt to take up as much space as possible. This means potential stretching. To avoid this, be sure to put the image inside a container such as a `<div>` element that has a width already set.

This will make all your images fit the screen they are viewed on, but it does nothing for file size. On top of the included file size, using large images and forcing the browser to scale can be CPU and memory intensive. That might not matter too much with your desktop or laptop computer, but it quickly becomes a very real problem when looking at rendering speed and power consumption on a mobile device.

> ### Tip
> If you are currently using image maps on your site, you will need to come up with a new solution. Because of the pixel-perfect mapping of image maps, images that are resized will no longer have targets in the places you expect. You can work around this by positioning invisible hot spots on the image by using a percentage for layout, but this is far from a bulletproof solution.

I do not advocate the use of browser-resized images by giving the browser a large image and forcing it to handle scaling the displayed size as a standard practice in your design; however, it can be a last-minute solution to get you by until you can get the correct images or solution in place.

Using Intrinsic Ratio

Maybe this has happened to you: You're browsing the web and start to load a page, but as you begin reading, the content is suddenly moved or shoved in a new direction as images are loaded. This is called page reflow and is caused by images being loaded in a place that did not already adjust the layout to handle them. Figure 9.5 shows a page before and after images are loaded, to illustrate this effect.

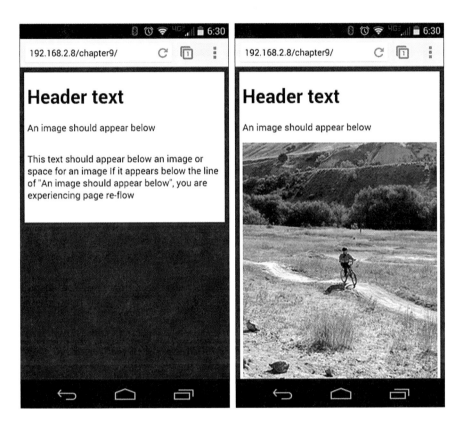

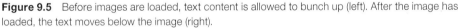

Figure 9.5 Before images are loaded, text content is allowed to bunch up (left). After the image has loaded, the text moves below the image (right).

You might be thinking, "Well, of course the text moved! I can't define how the space of an image changes on every screen!" That's true, you definitely cannot. However, if you know the ratio of that image, you can use a little trick to determine how much space the image will take up in this particular layout.

Thierry Koblentz first talked about the intrinsic ratio on A List Apart in 2009 (http://alistapart. com/article/creating-intrinsic-ratios-for-video/). In the article, Thierry talks about using the intrinsic ratio for handling videos on websites. It also happens to work quite well for images that need to use a placeholder to stop page reflow.

To see this in action, Figure 9.6 shows the same page, but with a plan for the page reflow by including space for the image by using the intrinsic ratio of the image. This is noticeable in comparison to Figure 9.5 because the text "This text should appear below..." is not visible on the screen when the page initially loads; instead, you only see the "An image should appear below" as the page has now saved space to insert the image.

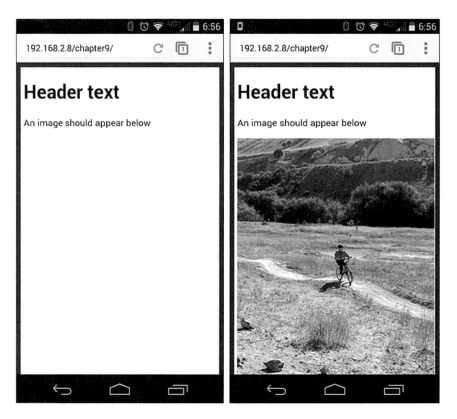

Figure 9.6 Space has been reserved (left) for the image to load into (right).

To figure out the intrinsic ratio, you need to know the aspect ratio of your image, divide the second number by the first, and use the result as padding on a container element.

For example, if you have a 480x320px image, the aspect ratio is 3:2. Taking that ratio, you get the value of 2/3, or 66.67. With this number, you can now set up a container element that will be used as a placeholder for the image. The CSS looks like this:

```
.wrapper {
  position: relative;
  padding-bottom: 66.67%;
  height: 0;
}
.image {
  position: absolute;
  top: 0;
  left: 0;
  width: 100%;
  height: 100%;
}
```

When using intrinsic ratios, you need to create multiple classes for each aspect ratio you use with your images. This way, you can have differently sized images and still have placeholders for them.

The `srcset` Attribute

If you have rather sanely decided that scaling images is not something you'd like to pursue, you might be interested in using the `srcset` attribute.

This attribute is used with the `img` element and is quite elegant in the execution of choosing the correct image to display.

Look at the following snippet:

```
<img src="meh.jpg" alt="an image" />
```

Yes, that is the ordinary way to add an image to your site. It has an `src` attribute that specifies which file to use (in this case, the aptly named `meh.jpg`), and the `alt` attribute enables you to add text that will appear if the image is unavailable, for text readers, and for similar uses.

The following snippet has had the `srcset` attribute added:

```
<img src="standard.jpg"
    alt="an image"
    srcset="small_480.jpg 480w,
            standard_768.jpg 768w,
            large_1024.jpg 1024w,
            large@2x.jpg 2x" />
```

> ### Tip
> Use a naming convention with your images. The previous snippet of `srcset` uses a bit of humor to help convey that you can use larger images with more detail as the screen gets larger, but you should not copy those naming standards. Attempting to manage a large number of files with names that do not match will be tricky and, in the long run, not worth the stress. Using names such as `hero_480.jpg` and `hero_480@2x.jpg` is a much better system.

You can see from the previous example snippet that the `srcset` attribute takes a list of comma-separated values. They might seem a little out of sorts at first, but at second glance, you should notice that there is a value ending with `w` after almost every image filename. That value tells the browser the size or limit of showing that image.

That breaks down into the following:

- 0–480px screens will show `small_480.jpg`.
- 481–768px screens will show `standard_768.jpg`.
- 769–1024px screens will show `large_1024.jpg`.
- High-pixel-density screens will show `large@2x.jpg`.
- All other screens will use `standard.jpg`.

This is a fantastic solution, but use it with careful planning to make sure that you are serving optimized images to the correct devices. Having a fallback image is nice, but it could leave you with an image that is either too small or too large to fit the device that triggered the fallback.

You might also want to be careful when using the element because it has been implemented only in WebKit-based browsers and Chrome 34+.

With a little luck, other browsers will start supporting the attribute soon. If you find that you cannot contain your excitement and you need to use it now, you or your developer can use a polyfill (https://github.com/borismus/srcset-polyfill) to fill in the gap and start using `srcset` now.

The `picture` Element

Another proposed solution for responsive images is a new element that will be used in concert with the `img` element. The goal of this element is to provide a way for images to be displayed based on device specifics and media queries.

Listing 9.1 demonstrates how the `picture` element could be implemented into a site.

Listing 9.1 Using the `picture` Element

```
01 <picture>
02   <source srcset="small.jpg">
03   <source media="(min-width: 480px)" srcset="mid.jpg 1x, mid@2x.jpg 2x">
04   <source media="(min-width: 768px)" srcset="large.jpg">
05   <img src="default.jpg" alt="The image">
06 </picture>
```

The way the `picture` element works is really quite fascinating. The element acts as a wrapper that uses `source` elements as well as an `img` element. Use of the `img` element helps browsers that do not currently support the `picture` element render an image.

The `source` element is used for setting up parameters that define what image should be rendered. On line 2, the `srcset` attribute is used to define an image that will be displayed on screens that measure from 0px and up. It does not cover all screen sizes because of the `source` elements that are defined on lines 3 and 4.

On line 3, you can see that a `media` attribute has been used to define the image that devices with a minimum screen size of 480px will render. It also contains the `srcset` attribute that defines a high-pixel-density image if the device supports it.

Looking ahead to line 4, you can see that the `media` attribute has been used again to define what image devices with a minimum screen resolution of 768px will see.

To break this down, the images will display as follows:

- Devices with a screen width of 0–479px will load `small.jpg`.
- Devices with a screen width of 480–767px will load either `mid.jpg` or `mid@2x.jpg`, depending on pixel density.
- Devices with a minimum width of 768px will load `large.jpg`.
- Browsers that do not support the `picture` element will load `default.jpg`.

It might also be somewhat surprising to see the `srcset` attribute inside the `source` element or even find it supported. It is actually encouraged to help deliver the proper image to the browser.

There is more to using the `picture` element than just specifying which images to use and using media queries to decide. You can also do some limited feature support testing with it to deliver images based on the browser supporting the image format.

You might be thinking that if a browser is "modern" enough to support the `picture` element, then it surely must have support for all picture formats. I can easily see why you might have gone down that path in your thinking, but you need to remember that not all browsers support the WEBP image format yet (for a current list, visit http://caniuse.com/webp).

Using the `type` attribute, you can specify whether an image should be displayed based on browser support. Listing 9.2 shows how this is possible.

Listing 9.2   Specifying Different Animated Image Formats

```
01 <picture>
02   <source type="image/webp" srcset="funny.webp">
03   <source type="video/png" srcset="funny.apng">
04   <img src="funny.gif" alt="absolute madness" />
05 </picture>
```

Looking closely at Listing 9.2, you can see that the `type` attribute is used on lines 2 and 3. On line 2, it contains a value of `image/webp`, and line 3 contains a value of `video/png`. Unless you are the type of designer who regularly tweaks your web server, these values might appear to be utter nonsense. These values are known as a MIME type.

The server and browser use the MIME type to communicate and describe the file that is being transferred and rendered. The `image/webp` value explains that the file is an image of the WEBP variety. The browser already has a list of known MIME types and decides whether it should use that file. The value of `video/png` might appear wrong, but that is the valid MIME type for animated PNG files.

Chrome supports the WEBP image format (including animated WEBP files), but Firefox does not. Firefox does support animated PNG files, however, and other browsers support animated GIF files.

By using the `picture` element to specify which image to use, you can optimize the experience for mobile and desktop users.

At the time of this writing, the `picture` element is not currently supported in any browser. However, there is a project underway for both Firefox and Chrome browsers to have support implemented hopefully before the end of 2014.

To learn more about the `picture` element, including how to load multiple images for multiple sizes in a more streamlined fashion, visit http://picture.responsiveimages.org/.

Using a JavaScript Solution

Designers and developers who are unable to work with modern browsers, or who do not have the time for the rest of the world to catch up with technology, will be using a JavaScript solution as part of their progressive enhancement suite.

Picturefill, from Scott Jehl, has seen excellent success. I have also created and used my own solution, called Pixity, on several projects.

Picturefill

The problem with the `picture` element is that, if you want to use it now, you can't. Even with browsers adding support for it in the near future, you are bound to users actually using that particular browser and having it work on their mobile devices.

This is the problem Scott Jehl saw, so he decided to implement a JavaScript solution that is based on the `picture` element but uses `span` elements to allow it to work safely cross-browser.

Note that Picturefill works best with browsers that support CSS3 media queries. With most smartphones, this should not pose a problem because almost all support CSS3 today.

Listing 9.3 shows the HTML markup needed to use Picturefill in your project.

Listing 9.3   Specifying Different Animated Image Formats

```
01 <span data-picture data-alt="description of image">
02   <span data-src="small.jpg"></span>
03   <span data-src="medium.jpg" data-media="(min-width: 480px)"></span>
04   <span data-src="large.jpg" data-media="(min-width: 768px)"></span>
05   <span data-src="extralarge.jpg" data-media="(min-width: 1140px)"></span>
06
07   <noscript>
08       <img src="small.jpg" alt="description of image">
09   </noscript>
10 </span>
```

Lines 2–5 show the initial setup required to make Picturefill work on browsers that support JavaScript, and lines 7–9 show the image that will be shown on devices that do not support JavaScript.

Line 1 uses data attributes of `data-picture` and `data-alt` Picturefill uses to determine where the image will be placed and what text will be used as the image's alternate message for screen readers and similar devices.

The other lines contain at least a data attribute of `data-src`. Others have an accompanying `data-media` that specifies the image that should be used and the requirements for displaying that particular image.

If you review both the `srcset` and `picture` element sections, this should start looking very similar in execution. You might be wondering about high-pixel-density screens and how they fit into the equation. They are added by changing the media query in the `data-media` attribute. Let's copy and modify a line so that it will serve a high-density image. Note that I have broken the line out to make it easier to read:

```
<span
  data-src="medium@2x.jpg"
  data-media="(min-width: 480px) and (min-device-pixel-ratio: 2.0)">
</span>
```

This could now be added as line 4, and support for high-pixel-density devices would be added for devices between 480px and 767px wide.

To download Picturefill and read the full usage guide, visit https://github.com/scottjehl/picturefill.

Pixity

Before I saw Picturefill, I was working on a redesign of an eCommerce site that now has more than 40% mobile users.

Knowing that the site is somewhere between 60% and 70% images, I needed a solution that gave me the flexibility of serving different files to different screen sizes but also allowed the content manager an easy way to specify images without having development constantly hard-coding the images into the dynamic files.

The solution was to create a plugin called Pixity. The first use of the plugin was actually to specify when to use high-pixel-density images; that is where the name originated, the PIXel densITY.

Pixity currently is released as a jQuery (1.7+) plugin and is fairly easy to implement. By adding a few data attributes to an `img` element and giving the image a specific class, the Pixity plugin runs on page load and replaces a small 1x1 pixel image with the appropriate image for the device.

Listing 9.4 demonstrates the HTML markup of an image using Pixity.

Listing 9.4   Using Pixity to Display an Image

```
<img class="pixity"
  src="images/placeholder.gif"
  alt="image description"
  data-path="images/"
  data-sm="small.jpg"
  data-md="medium.jpg"
  data-lg="large.jpg"
  data-xl="xlarge.jpg" />
```

Unlike Picturefill and `srcset`, you do not specify the minimum device widths for your images. Instead, they are predefined.

By default, the sizes for the images used are as follows:

- `data-sm`: 0–480px
- `data-md`: 481–767px
- `data-lg`: 768–959px
- `data-xl`: 960px+

You can change the defaults by modifying the jQuery call like so:

```
$.pixity({limitSm:600,limitMd:960,limitLg,1280});
```

Note the `data-path` attribute. This attribute might seem a bit out of place, but it is quite use-ful with a CMS system with a limited amount of characters. If you are using a CDN with a long directory path, instead of putting it in for every image, you put it in once and then fine-tune it with the other data attributes.

> **Tip**
>
> When using Pixity, you should use an intrinsic ratio if at all possible. Because of the use of a small placeholder image, failing to use an intrinsic ratio will cause the page to reflow on the user.

If you are interested in modifying and editing JavaScript, you can modify and extend Pixity to fit your needs. I have several versions that have not been uploaded to GitHub that I use to work with loading dynamic and responsive content into sliders, and one version allows the client to download the high-pixel-density version of a file only if the client passes a speed test.

Pixity Core is currently licensed as MIT (http://opensource.org/licenses/MIT) and is available for download and modification at https://github.com/dutsonpa/pixity.

Summary

In this chapter, you learned that displaying images takes planning and care. By taking the time to fine-tune the images that will be displayed to users, you increase the chance of them using and returning to your site.

You learned that you can take advantage of art direction to change the visual message you are sharing. You can do this with some new features, such as the `srcset` attribute, or by taking advantage of JavaScript plugins such as Picturefill and Pixity.

CHAPTER 10

RESPONSIVE VIDEO

When you want to inform, entertain, and give a broad overview with a semi-captive audience, using a video is a great way to communicate your message. If you can get your video to be shared socially or "go viral," you can be sure you're on the right track, and your campaign will definitely see the boost.

How you handle the playback of your video, however, can either keep people coming back or break your campaign apart. In this chapter, you learn about video as a medium and how to make sure that it plays back on as many devices as possible.

Using Video

The way mobile users act is a rather fascinating subject. When it comes to searching or browsing a site, they have little patience for a bad interface; and if they can find the information or product somewhere else, they won't hesitate to leave your site and go there instead. However, when it comes to using social networks, video-sharing sites, and entertainment hubs, they will happily waste minutes to hours to get the content they want.

People love to share things. They love to be first and to get credit for being the first to pin, plus, like, share, or mention something. This why using a video can be what tips the balance in making a user complete a purchase.

Even if the product isn't something you currently need, or even something you were thinking of purchasing, watching a video makes you more likely to think of it and could increase the odds of your completing a purchase later.

An interesting development that has swept social media sharing is the advent of sharable short videos. Popular social applications such as Vine and Instagram both feature short videos as a means of sharing. This doesn't mean you should be making 5- to 15-second videos, but it does mean that there is a demand for fast, easy-to-share videos.

As with standard site performance, with videos, the faster you can deliver the message the better it is going to be received. In this regard, it is very important that you use a quality provider or else have a content delivery network (CDN) provider that can keep pace with your distribution and demand.

> ## Tip
> Using a CDN has the potential to speed up your content delivery. This is accomplished by hosting your content on multiple servers in various parts of the world. Whenever a user requests an asset from the CDN, the server closest to the user responds and sends the asset. The greater the distance from a user to your content, the bigger the benefit of using a CDN. Several popular CDN providers that you might want to take a look at are Akamai, CloudFlare, MaxCDN, and Limelight Networks.

Delivery Systems

You can use a variety of ways to get the videos from your server to the device your consumer is using. The price of doing this varies considerably based on the features you need to accomplish your distribution goals.

Before deciding on a content provider, you need to consider the following:

- Available bitrate
- Device-specific playback
- HTML5 versus Flash player
- CDN availability
- Minimum transfer speed
- File size constraints
- Social sharing options
- Player customization
- Video protection, including region and domain locking
- Ad integration support

Knowing what your needs are up front will save you from an expensive contract and from not getting the features that you need.

Limelight Networks

Limelight Networks (www.limelight.com/) is a content delivery network (CDN) that provides services for content, application, and video delivery. It provides a solution that is geared toward enterprise users, but I have found the staff to be friendly and willing to help meet your personal needs.

Key features of using Limelight Networks for video distribution include these:

- Worldwide CDN to distribute video
- HTML5 video playback available
- Domain locking for content available
- FTP video upload
- Branded video player
- Video player with available bandwidth detection
- Transcoding services available
- iOS friendly
- Video analytics
- Advertisement support
- Social sharing options
- Playlist support
- Custom content channel creation

Being able to change the bitrate of the video streaming to the device viewing the video is important because it allows users to spend less time buffering and more time watching your content. Limelight is a very competitive solution that is actively improving its services to exceed the offerings of its competitors. The Limelight website does not offer pricing information, but signing up for a free trial gets you in touch with a representative who will be more than happy to customize a plan to fit your needs.

Akamai

Akamai (www.akamai.com/) has a reputation of being a world leader in web distribution services. It attained this reputation by providing fast, reliable services. The Sola part of the Akamai family is exclusively focused on video storage, delivery, and protection. With many offered services, the bulk of Akamai's services lean toward the enterprise user who is looking for subscription or providers who need content protected from content thieves.

Some of the key features of Akamai Sola are as follows:

- Distribution from the Akamai CDN
- Domain and region lock, as well as DRM services
- Adaptive bitrate playback
- Multiple protocol support, including HLS, HDS, and MPEG-DASH
- Media analytics
- Advertisement support

Akamai is in the same category as Limelight Networks, so getting a price is heavily geared toward working with a representative that will customize the service to your needs.

Brightcove

One of the newer video content providers, Brightcove, has radically evolved in the past few years from a simple content provider to one of the leading-edge video distributors. It offers a product called Video Cloud with a varied pricing model that works for everyone from small business to mammoth enterprise users. As a premier leader, it offers many of the same features as other competitors.

Key features of Brightcove Video Cloud include these:

- Transcoding services
- Media analytics
- Custom players
- HTML5 playback support

- Mobile device support
- Bandwidth and bitrate detection
- Bulk upload transcoding service
- Capability to schedule and synchronize video upload to YouTube channels
- Advertising support
- Domain, region, and DRM support (RMTPe and SWF)

Because this is a newer service, you might have reservations about the quality and reliability of service. However, I have used Brightcove on projects over the last three years and have found that it readily meets the demands of users and also constantly upgrades and improves its current offerings. It has a helpful support staff and is quick to reply to emails and calls. If you are seriously looking into adding video playback into your site, Brightcove is worth your consideration.

Vimeo

Vimeo (https://vimeo.com/) has fought a considerable battle against formidable foes such as YouTube. That doesn't mean Vimeo is tired and ready to hang up the towel, though. On the contrary, it is rolling out new features, support, and plans for meeting even the most demanding video sites.

As one of the first sites to allow user-uploaded videos that could go beyond the 10-minute mark without a special seal of approval, Vimeo has gained a reputation for hosting strikingly visual masterpieces that are more akin to a fully funded production effort than user-produced videos.

Features available with Vimeo are as follows:

- Embeddable video
- Customizable branded video player*
- Video groups
- Video channels
- Video albums
- Analytics*
- Domain-restricted videos*
- Vimeo On Demand*
- Transcoded video

*Plus or Pro subscription required

Multiple account types are available, and each has a slightly richer feature set. If you are a business user, Vimeo is worth looking at because it has reasonable storage limits and one of the best bandwidth policies of most video-streaming services. Also a plus for those who would like to sell videos, the Vimeo On Demand feature allows you to sell your content.

YouTube

YouTube has been the creative and quick-to-video outlet for the masses of people on the Internet who want to be discovered, share something amazing, or quickly share a video with friends and family.

YouTube has continued to roll out new features, including an HTML5 video player and mobile device support, and it is the engine behind videos embedded into Google+.

The popular features of YouTube are as follows:

- Free with Google account sign-up
- Embeddable videos
- Transcoded video
- Bandwidth detection and adjustment
- Channel support
- Integration with Google+ and Google Search
- Limited advertisement support

YouTube is a popular platform to use because it is available at one of my favorite prices: free. It also handles much of the heavy lifting, including adding ads to your videos to help generate revenue, and will create multiple versions of your video for playback on most devices. The cost of all of this is the fact that, when your video is finished playing, you get a wall of "similar" videos that might show questionable content or direct your viewers to another product or service or an unflattering review of your brand. That is not to say that you shouldn't still leverage the power and influence of YouTube—just be sure to consider the cons before committing to using it as your only streaming provider.

Making Videos Fit Mobile Devices

After you decide on a service to use as your video provider and you upload your video, it is time to add the video to your page.

Unfortunately, when it comes to mobile devices, this is not a simple plug-and-play process. Figure 10.1 shows what happens when a video that has not been optimized for mobile devices is played back on a mobile device.

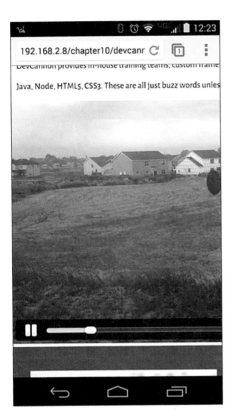

Figure 10.1 The video is not properly sized for the screen.

This doesn't completely stop users from enjoying the video, though, and they should have the option to make the video go full screen.

Another problem that you might face is launching the video into a modal. Figure 10.2 shows a possible issue when using video playback with a modal window.

Figure 10.2 shows a terrible UI. Even worse, the user might not be able to close the modal without reloading the page, touching the Back button, or leaving your site.

Using Intrinsic Ratio

With both the issues shown in Figure 10.1 and 10.2, the video player is not properly sized to the device. You can solve this by using the same intrinsic ratio logic used in dealing with responsive images. To see how this works, consider an example YouTube video.

Figure 10.2 The modal window is bigger than the screen viewing it, making the video—and, more importantly, the Close button—completely inaccessible. It also is confusing because a user might have no idea why the screen has gone almost completely black, with no way to start or stop the video.

If you have ever used the embed code from YouTube, you should recognize the following:

```
<iframe
width="640"
height="360"
src="//www.youtube.com/embed/yXXZSbx2lrc"
frameborder="0"
allowfullscreen></iframe>
```

Nothing is wrong with the `iframe` code, per se; however, it does not contain any code to help the video fit the device that is viewing it. Figure 10.3 demonstrates how the video is viewed on a mobile device.

Figure 10.3   Even though the site is responsive, the embedded video is not and breaks out of frame.

> **Tip**
>
> Remember that when using an intrinsic ratio, you need to know the aspect ratio of the video. Generally, most videos have an aspect ratio of 4:3, 3:2, or 16:9.
>
> If you need to figure out the aspect ratio of your video, you will need the pixel values for the width and height of your video. You can then use a ratio calculator to get the aspect ratio that will be used to figure out the intrinsic ratio. A calculator is available to help you figure out the intrinsic and aspect ratios at www.mobiledesignrecipes.com/ratio-calculator/.

To make this work, you need to add the HTML for a container that you can use to attach the intrinsic ratio to:

```
<div class="video-wrapper">
  <iframe
      class="video"
```

```
       width="640"
       height="360"
       src="//www.youtube.com/embed/yXXZSbx2lrc"
       frameborder="0"
       allowfullscreen></iframe>
</div>
```

Note that the formatting of the code has been changed for readability; otherwise, the entire iframe element would be on one line. Now that the HTML has been taken care of, you need to add the styles that will make the video scale to fit the screen:

```
.video-wrapper {
  position: relative;
  padding-bottom: 56.25%;
  height: 0;
}
.video {
  position: absolute;
  top: 0;
  left: 0;
  width: 100%;
  height: 100%;
}
```

In this CSS snippet, the intrinsic ratio is used to set up the padding-bottom value. The current value of 56.25% works for videos with an aspect ratio of 16:9. Depending on the aspect ratio of your video, you need to change this value. To determine the value you should use, you can use the ratio calculator at www.mobiledesignrecipes.com/ratio-calculator/.

With the HTML and CSS in place, the video should now scale to fit the device viewing it. Figure 10.4 shows the video playing back on a mobile device.

Using the Native Player

Another option to consider is having your video play in the native video player of the device. Using the native player offers many benefits, including these:

- Users are more likely to understand how the player works.
- Lower bitrates can be used for more device compatibility.
- Video can be streamed without a third-party service.

Using the native player is triggered by serving a "native" file to the device. This can be done by linking directly to the file, using a shortened URL, or even using a QR code that forwards directly to a video.

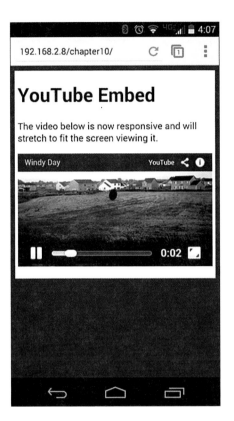

Figure 10.4 The size of the video now changes to match the size of the screen that is viewing it.

To see this in action for yourself, open the browser on your mobile device and go to http://goo.gl/rqlkHC.

> ### Tip
> If you decide to use a short URL or a QR code, it is important that you strongly consider using a landing page to launch or watch the video. This gives users some-thing to read or look at while they wait for the video to download, buffer, and start playback. Try using the link http://goo.gl/B4t9ry to see what a landing page could look like instead of launching directly to the native player.

If you do not happen to have your mobile device available, the link also works in any browser that can play back MP4-encoded videos, such as Chrome. Figure 10.5 shows what the native player on an Android device looks like.

Figure 10.5   The video is displayed full screen, and the Play/Pause button as well as the scrubbing controls are currently visible.

Using a Plugin

If you decide that you do not want to handle figuring out any ratios or cluttering up your styles with extra entries, you might want to opt for a JavaScript plugin.

One of my favorite plugins for handling responsive video is FitVids.js (http://fitvidsjs.com/). This is a jQuery plugin that can be used with popular video-sharing sites such as YouTube and Vimeo.

The implementation of FitVids.js is beyond the scope of this chapter, but I can tell you that it is a simple plugin to incorporate into your site. For documentation, including how to incorporate FitVids.js into your site, visit the GitHub site at https://github.com/davatron5000/FitVids.js/.

Summary

In this chapter, you learned about why using video in your site matters, and you discovered some providers that you can leverage for content delivery.

You also learned why responsive videos are important and how to make them responsive on your site. This is accomplished by using the intrinsic ratio, the native device player, or a plugin such as FitVids.js.

CHAPTER 11

IMAGE COMPRESSION

When it comes to the visual brilliance of design, file formats might not be the first thing you think of. In fact, it might not even register as something you need to think about at all. When working with mobile devices, the file type you use can mean the difference between happy users who love your site and users who are just happy they can find the information elsewhere.

In this chapter, you learn about image file types, including when best to use each format, and you learn about various compression options to make sure you give users an optimized experience.

Image Types

Depending on the job you have, you might have some familiarity with various image file types. You might already know that most cameras and smartphones take pictures in the JPEG format. You might also be familiar with OS X and know that taking screenshots will output PNG files.

You are also undoubtedly aware that using various image-manipulation programs, such as Adobe Photoshop, Pixelmator, Acorn, and GIMP, enable you to save images in a variety of formats.

What you might not know is when you should use each format, or even why so many different formats are available.

JPEG/JPG

The JPEG, or JPG, image format is a common lossy format that is used primarily in digital photography. When you take a picture with your tablet, smartphone, or digital-SLR, there is an extremely good chance that your image will be saved as a JPEG image.

> **Note**
>
> Images are saved in either a lossless or a lossy format. Some image containers, such as PNG, offer both lossless and lossy saving options. When an image is saved as lossless, all information to display that image is retained. When a lossy format, such as JPEG, is used to save an image, calculations are made that reduce the overall size of the image, but at the cost of destroying the original data. The new image has new data; if edited and saved again in a lossy format, it will lose more detail. This process adds distortion, loss of color, and diminished clarity, and it can add artifacts to the image.

JPEG images can be saved at various quality levels that change both the information contained inside the image and the overall file size. The compression used in JPEG files is beneficial because, even in Photoshop, saving a file at the High setting saves the file at around 60% quality. Figure 11.1 illustrates how the same file appears at two different quality levels.

As you can see, the higher the quality setting, the sharper the image and the less "artifacting" that's visible in the final image.

Figure 11.1   An image saved at the highest quality setting (left) appears different from one saved at the lowest (right).

> **Tip**
>
> JPEG files can be saved normally or can be saved as an interlaced format called progressive. The progressive format might be slightly larger, but when rendered on a web page, it gives the illusion of loading quickly because it makes several "passes" as it is drawn. This tricks the mind into believing that the page is loading fast, and it helps eliminate page reflow because some of the image is displayed as it is downloaded.

As a designer, you should use JPEG images any time that you need large images or images with hundreds or more colors. Anytime you are displaying something with a complex color scheme (such as skin), you should be using a JPEG.

Because the file size of your JPEG image is determined by the information contained in the image, you can decrease file size and increase visual guidance by blurring or desaturating areas of an image to reduce the data needed to replicate thousands of accurately reproduced pixels. Figure 11.2 demonstrates how this is accomplished and the effects of doing so.

Consider some other facts about the JPEG image format:

- JPEG files have a maximum resolution of 65535x65535.
- Because of the lossy format, repeatedly editing and saving a JPEG file will cause degradation over time. Always keep an original for editing instead of editing a copy of a copy.
- Currently, all modern and most legacy browsers support JPEG files.

Figure 11.2 By blurring and desaturating the background (top), the focus is clearly on the subject and the file size is decreased to 36KB from 108KB when compared to the original (bottom).

GIF

The Graphics Interchange Format (GIF) tends to instantly conjure up one of two things: Either you are a user who instantly thinks about funny cats, stupid tricks, or both in short, no-sound videos, or you think of transparent logos or low-color images.

The GIF format starting seeing use from CompuServe in 1987, and it very quickly ruled the entire landscape of pretty much all GeoCities websites (don't try to pretend you don't remember—I know that you still have nightmares about those heady days). These were the times of simple looping animation, and it was just about the only way to add a little special something into the fledgling web.

GIF files serve a greater purpose than just allowing users to view short clips, spinning globes, or even page loaders. The GIF file is perfect for use with single- or few-color items, such as logo images. For comparison, Figure 11.3 shows a GIF file and a JPEG file.

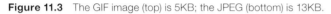

Figure 11.3   The GIF image (top) is 5KB; the JPEG (bottom) is 13KB.

GIF files also support transparency, which is a wonderful feature, but this does come at a cost: The image must have a stroke applied that matches the background, or the images will appear chipped or blocky around the transparent areas. Figure 11.4 demonstrates the use of transparency with a GIF file.

Figure 11.4   Both images are transparent; however, the one on the right has a stroke applied, making it appear without jagged edges

Consider some other facts about GIF files:

- GIF files support a 256-color palette.
- GIF files use LZW lossless compression.
- GIF is officially pronounced like Jif, the peanut butter brand.
- All modern and most legacy browsers support GIF files.

PNG

Thanks to the deficiencies in the GIF file format (not to mention problems with licensing agreements between Unisys and CompuServe), the Portable Network Graphics (PNG) format was created.

The goal of the PNG format was to become not only the replacement of the GIF image format, but the main image format used on the Internet.

With PNG, almost everything you would want in an image format is present. PNG contains much better transparency support than GIF, and it has a very wide colorspace, allowing you to save images with the same amount of color as in JPEG.

In fact, if you find yourself creating any type of pattern or gradient with a JPEG, you will see sharper results by switching to PNG. This is because of the accurate color reproduction and the lossless compression. JPEG files will have some degree of artifacting present.

A trick you can use when saving PNG files is to use Posterize in Photoshop. Posterizing your image reduces the number of tones in your image. If you apply too much of the effect, your image will lose fine details and depth. To do this, edit your image and then choose Image -> Adjustments -> Posterize from the File menu. The fewer levels you use, the smaller the image will be. When posterizing your image, it is important that you inspect your image, or you might end up losing some detail. Figure 11.5 demonstrates the files and savings of using this technique.

Figure 11.5   The original image (left) is 18KB, and the posterized image (right) is 16KB.

The difference between each image is extremely subtle. This shows the effectiveness of posterizing your images to save file size and still be able to display a high-quality image. Note that the image also contains transparent areas. Unlike in GIF images, these areas do not have jagged edges, but are instead displayed smooth.

Consider some other facts about the PNG file:

- All modern browsers support PNG files, but not all legacy ones support transparency.
- Even though PNG is a newer format, GIF files can still be smaller on some images.

- PNG files use lossless file compression, enabling you to edit and save the same file over and over without worrying about data loss.

- PNG files can be animated (APNG), but browser support is very limited and is a safe bet only when working with Firefox.

WebP

One of the newest image formats available is WebP. This format has a deep history in video compression from the VP8 codec. It was constructed using technology originally developed by On2 and is now championed by Google. Utilities to convert and compress images into WebP are available at https://developers.google.com/speed/webp/. Some image-manipulation programs also include support to export in this format. Pixelmator (www.pixelmator.com/) is one of these programs.

The WebP format is similar to the PNG format, in that it allows a very high number of colors and transparency support. This makes WebP suitable for use as a JPEG, GIF, and PNG replacement.

WebP files offer some fantastic gains in reducing file size, and with very little (if any) visual disturbance. Figure 11.6 demonstrates the differences among various image formats.

Figure 11.6 Not only is there very little difference in each format, but WebP is the smallest of all.

It is worth noting the file sizes of each of the images shown in Figure 11.6:

- **PNG:** 153KB
- **GIF:** 42KB
- **JPEG:** 30KB
- **WebP:** 18KB

The savings WebP offers are not only considerable, but are lifesaving when considering the image payload you are sending to your mobile users.

Consider some other facts about WebP:

- WebP images can be animated like GIF files.
- WebP offers both lossy and lossless compression.
- The maximum resolution of a WebP file is 16384×16384.
- Browser support for WebP is limited to Chrome and Opera browsers (see http://caniuse.com/webp for updated support).

Compression Utilities

Knowing the type of image format to use is half the battle, as a popular 1980s cartoon would say. The other half comes from using various compression utilities.

In more than one meeting, I have literally dropped the jaws of those attending when I have taken the images from their site and, while discussing site strategy, shown them that their images are 10% to 25% too large.

How was I able to do this? By using the correct tools and adding a measure of corrective judgment. Let me show you the tools I use on a regular basis.

JPEGmini

JPEGmini (www.jpegmini.com/) is both a web service and an application. It works by optimizing the parts of a JPEG image that take up space but are not seen by your eyes. Note that this service works best with images taken with your DSLR or digital camera. If you use it with images that have already been compressed, the savings will be much less substantial. This sounds a little far-fetched, but if you give the service a try, you will find yourself pleasantly surprised.

The web service is easy to use. Start by visiting www.jpegmini.com/main/shrink_photo and then drag a photo from your computer into your browser (or use the upload image feature). Your image will then be processed and the new image will appear, along with technical data about how much space was saved.

If you run a design house, you might be interested in using the server technology JPEGmini provides to autoprocess your images in a batch process.

Two versions of the desktop application are available for Windows and OS X. The differences between them are the size of the files that can be processed, the speed of processing, and whether you need an Adobe Lightroom plugin.

PNGGauntlet

PNGGauntlet (http://pnggauntlet.com/) is a Windows application that compresses PNG files.

If you have ever worked with PNG file compression, you might have heard of PNGOUT, OptiPNG, and DeflOpt. These optimization applications for PNG files help reduce file size while keeping quality. PNGGauntlet combines all three of these applications into one and lets you process your files with it.

In this easy-to-use application, you pick an output folder and then drag and drop images into the application (or use the Add Images button). The files will immediately start processing.

Occasionally, I have found that the application might seem like it is "freezing," but this is because of the intense math operations that the application is performing to process your images.

Radical Image Optimization Tool

Another one of the applications I use when I am developing on a Windows computer is the Radical Image Optimization Tool (RIOT).

RIOT (http://luci.criosweb.ro/riot/) is available as either a standalone Windows application or a plugin that works with other image-manipulation programs, such as GIMP (www.gimp.org/).

This application is one of my favorite image utilities because it works with JPEG, GIF, and PNG files. It uses a dual-pane view so that you can visually compare your compression changes with the original file instead of using the "guess, optimize, repeat" approach that command-line and similar utilities often leave you with.

RIOT also contains more than just compression options. You can change masking, levels, color, and a slew of options based on the image format.

ImageAlpha

ImageAlpha (http://pngmini.com/) is my favorite PNG compression utility. This application runs on OS X and is available for free.

The magic behind ImageAlpha is that it takes a lossless 24-bit PNG image (or any PNG file) and changes the compression to lossy and the colorspace to 8-bit. This affects your ability to edit the image over and over (due to the lossy compression), but for most production images, this shouldn't be a problem.

Personally, I use ImageAlpha as part of a manual process. This gives me the opportunity to review the images and make sure I am getting the most compression with the least amount of visual disturbance.

An example workflow follows:

1. Save the PNG file in Adobe Photoshop using the Save for Web feature and choosing the PNG-24 preset.
2. Open ImageAlpha and make adjustments using the preview window to see what your changes look like.
3. Save the image and check the box to further process the image through ImageOptim.

By following this workflow, I saved 202KB (77%) from the original. Figure 11.7 shows both images side by side for comparison.

Figure 11.7   The original export is 264KB (left); the compressed file is 62KB (right).

Even if you are using automation, you can still get some incredible gains, but I strongly recommend reviewing files manually to make sure you are getting the best compression without sacrificing excessive quality of your image.

ImageOptim

ImageOptim (http://imageoptim.com/) is my second-favorite image compression utility. This is another OS X–only application, and it works with PNG, GIF, and JPEG files.

In fact, it is a fancy application wrapper for PNGOUT, Zopfli, Pngcrush, AdvPNG, OptiPNG, JpegOptim, jpegrescan, jpegtran, and Gifsicle. You could run each of these tools by yourself, but why go to all that effort when ImageOptim does this for you?

Using ImageOptim with your images is as easy as opening the program and dragging the images you would like optimized into it. Note that it overwrites your originals, so you might want to make a new folder that contains the images you would like compressed and then use those files.

As mentioned earlier, ImageOptim works very well when used in tandem with ImageAlpha. I have even found it extremely useful on images that I have already compressed with JPEGmini.

If you have access to OS X, this is a must-have application for your toolkit.

TinyPNG

TinyPNG (https://tinypng.com/) started out as a fantastic website that works much like JPEG-mini. It allows users to upload PNG files and have them returned in a refined and optimized fashion.

Really, it comes down to quantization of your uploaded file, as well as changing bit depth for colors and mucking about with the transparency a bit. But the results are fantastic; you can save anywhere from 50% to 80% on file size.

A relatively new feature that TinyPNG has pushed is an accessible developer API. This might not seem like a big deal on the surface, but having the capability to leverage its compression service inside your own company or freelance tooling is an exciting prospect.

Another new feature it has available is a plugin for Adobe Photoshop. This affordable plugin adds a wider spectrum of PNG support to the program and enables you to export images as needed or in batch, all with the compression you would expect from using the online service.

Compression Results

Even choosing the right image format and compressing it properly might not be enough to get you to start doing it. Looking at the statistics of your site and seeing how much data you can save might just help tip the balance and get you to start using the right images. An interesting discovery by the web team at Etsy showed that adding just 160KB of images to the site increased the mobile bounce rate by 12% (http://programming.oreilly.com/2014/01/web-performance-is-user-experience.html).

You can start gathering information in multiple ways, but I find that the easiest way is to download and install a copy of Mozilla Firefox (www.mozilla.org/en-US/firefox/new/) and pick up the excellent Web Developer extension by Chris Pederick (http://chrispederick.com/work/web-developer/).

When you have those both installed, browse to the site you would like to audit. Auditing your own site will give you the best perspective, but you can always audit a competitor or someone who has a similar design or flow to what you have.

After you have arrived at the site, click Information and then click View Document Size in the Web Developer Toolbar. A new page should appear and display page statistics. Figure 11.8 shows the menu option and the results screen.

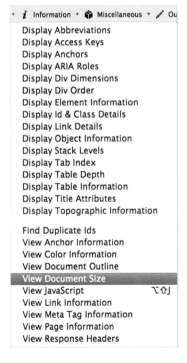

Figure 11.8 Click View Document Size (left) to get a generated report in a new tab (right).

As you can see from my report, I have 74 images on the page, which are taking up 429KB of space.

Of those 74 images, I have access to 49 of them, totaling 283.9KB. Figure 11.9 shows my results of running those 49 through ImageOptim.

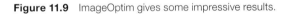

File	Size	Savings
1px_002.gif	43	0%
1px.gif	43	0%
130328113528–old-man-sneezing-allergies-bi...	6,325	7.1%
130430065839–wilcox-prom-jrotc-couple-vide...	3,683	10.4%
130604201305–home-page---must-watch-tv-...	3,250	10.2%
130604201308–home-page---must-watch-tv-...	3,557	10.4%
130604201314–home-page---must-watch-tv-...	3,575	10.0%
130627162800–new-dad-baby-shutterstock-bi...	5,193	7.7%
130801152726–wendy-sachs-headshot-video-t...	3,535	66.6%
130816155344–entt1–jim-parsons-video-tease.jpg	3,264	10.0%
140320162510–spc-vital-signs-3d-printing-gr...	5,406	7.1%
140326185423–03-scotland-castles-restricted–...	4,314	57.7%
140326185437–07-scotland-castles-restricted–...	6,797	68.3%

+   Saved 69.5KB out of 283.9KB. 24.5% overall (up to 85.2% per file)   ↻ Again

Figure 11.9 ImageOptim gives some impressive results.

As Figure 11.9 shows, I was able to shrink at least one image by 85.2%, and overall, I was able to save 24.5%, leaving me with 214KB worth of images instead of 253.9KB.

Remember that this was on just one page. If you can save even 10% across your entire site, that will get you one step closer to a successful site across any device and platform.

Summary

In this chapter, you learned about different image formats, as well as the appropriate time to use each one. You learned that the WebP format is an up-and-coming solution to delivering very flexible imagery with minimal file size.

You also learned about some very helpful tools that you can use on Windows or OS X, or on the web as a service. These tools and applications can help you get the most out of your images so that mobile users can enjoy them and see the beauty of your work.

You also saw an example of why serving these optimized files is essential for your mobile users.

PART III

ENHANCING PERFORMANCE

CHAPTER 12

CONDITIONAL JAVASCRIPT

Even when you have started mobile first with your design, paid careful attention to your content, and created a true masterpiece, you still need to worry about precise interaction methods. What works for your desktop users might not work at all for your mobile users. By that same token, what works on a tablet might not work on a phone. This is where adding some conditional JavaScript can make all the difference.

Why Conditional JavaScript

When you start thinking about how users will interact with your site, you need to make sure that you are giving them the control they expect to be successful. This holds true for every element or component of your site that will offer any degree of interaction.

To help wrap your head around user interactions with your site, think of how Android uses fragments to change what is displayed based on available screen sizes. Figure 12.1 demonstrates how Android fragments work.

Figure 12.1   Viewed in portrait orientation (left), the news stories appear as a list; viewed in landscape orientation (right), a list of news sources appears along with the news story.

In Figure 12.1, on the left, you see two news stories displayed, but no menu is visible to help navigate through the available stories. This is the view that would be shown on a phone. On the right side, you see what the app does when viewed on a tablet or widescreen device. Here the stories are moved to the right and reformatted, and a menu appears on the left to enable the user to navigate to different stories. The navigation and story display are different views or areas that are shown based on the screen size of the device.

Android uses fragments to do what you can accomplish with CSS media queries, and it exemplifies the need to look at your design from every possible angle. This includes elements such as sliders and image galleries, which are discussed next.

Sliders

Sliders are the bane of the developer and the boon of managers everywhere who want to cram just one more piece of content into an otherwise perfectly designed page.

Many considerations should go into the use of sliders:

- How big, in both dimensions and number of slides, is this going to be?
- Will mobile users be able to read the content?
- Will touchscreen users be able to control the slider with gestures?
- Should mobile users be forced to download the same content as desktop or similar users?

These questions are extremely important because they dictate the usability and also the impact the slider will have on the speed of your site. Unfortunately, you might find that the answer to some of these questions is much more complicated than you think.

For example, if you decide that you want to enable gestures for touchscreen devices, you need to make sure that your slider either has a high tolerance for swiping or has an aspect ratio that is not larger than the screen that is viewing it.

This is important because some sliders that offer gesture support will "scroll-jack" the swipe-down and prevent the user from moving any farther down the page. Figure 12.2 shows a mobile device viewing a slider that is too large.

Depending on your site, you can even opt to remove the slider altogether from small screens but show it on larger screens. This is an excellent way to conserve bandwidth on smaller devices and also avoid potential pitfalls with gesture-based scroll-jacking.

Other elements also need to be scrutinized for similar behaviors. Sometimes you will find that it is not as simple to decide how to replace a component of your site as it is to determine how to rearrange it.

Image Galleries

Image galleries represent almost every conceivable pain point you can have when dealing with a small-to-large screen solution. This isn't because image galleries are bad; it is because there is no unified way of displaying the information that all users are used to using.

Figure 12.2 The slider takes up too much space, giving a user no place to tap and swipe to move down the page or even realize that the image is part of a slider.

Here are some possible ways image galleries can be interacted with:

- Click or touch a thumbnail to change the main image.
- Click an image to view an even larger image in a modal window.
- Click any image or thumbnail to launch a modal window that has interaction points to load the next image or the previous image.
- Use a slider to show images.
- Use a combination of the previous methods, including showing extra-large images in a new window or tab.

Now that you are thinking about ways of interaction, let me throw in a twist. What if you have a design that uses a large image that dominates one side of the screen and then has the thumbnails and descriptive information on the other?

This is an acceptable option for larger screens and may be the solution you adopt on screens that are large enough to support it. However, on a mobile screen, either you will get an image that is so small you lose all detail, or you will have to juggle the page so that the image comes first and then the details and thumbnails come below. This is an acceptable option; however, you have to be careful with how the interaction is handled, or users will not see any changes when they tap thumbnails, leaving them frustrated. Figure 12.3 demonstrates some of the dangers that can occur.

Figure 12.3   The main image is visible with a decent amount of detail, but the thumbnails are nowhere to be found.

Figure 12.3 demonstrates a poor user interface because the user has to hunt for image thumbnails. Even if the user manages to find them, he or she might not notice any changes that occur while attempting to interact with them.

This is one of the major reasons you should consider using conditional JavaScript to augment your design.

Using Conditional JavaScript

Conditional JavaScript offers the capability to trigger plugins, functions, or methods when certain conditions are met.

If you think you have heard something like this before, you probably have. Another methodology that leans on this concept is progressive enhancement. This is the idea that you should find the absolute least common denominator and build up from there. This strategy is awesome because it will cover almost 100% of all devices, but it is also intensive and requires thorough testing and development.

For now, I show how you can create a function in JavaScript that you can use in a similar manner to a CSS media query. I also showcase some of the plugins that you can leverage in a similar fashion.

JavaScript Media Queries

CSS media queries use information passed from the browser to determine when to fire a certain set of styles.

To begin with conditional JavaScript, you need to do something similar: You need to find the size of the browser window. You can do this with the following code line:

```
var cw = document.body.clientWidth;
```

This particular snippet of code creates a variable named `cw` that will work with all modern browsers and several legacy ones, including the Android 2.3 browser.

Now that you can determine the width, here is an example of how you can use it inside your `script` block:

```
<script>
  var cw = document.body.clientWidth;
  if (cw > 750) {
    alert("You are using a tablet or bigger sized screen!");
  }
</script>
```

In the previous snippet, the screen width is determined. If it is at least 750px, a message appears informing users that they are using a tablet-size screen. Figure 12.4 shows a page with this script running on a phone and an iPad.

Now that you have seen a simple example, let's plunge into how a full-fledged script works. Listing 12.1 shows an extrapolated implementation of the simple example.

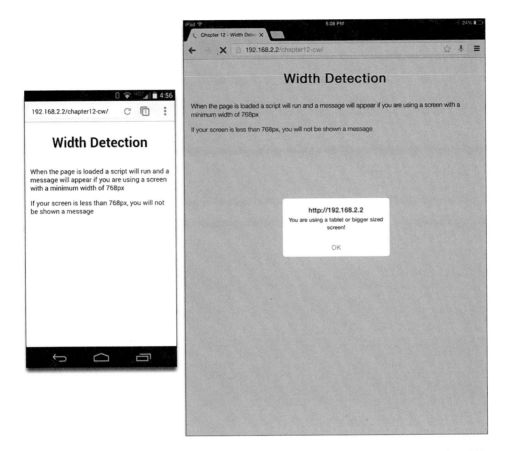

Figure 12.4   When the phone (left) loads the page, an alert message is not shown because the width is below 768; when the iPad (right) loads the page, the alert message is displayed.

Listing 12.1   Using JavaScript Conditionally Based on Screen Size

```
01 //Globals
02 var resize = null,
03   limitSm = 768,
04   limitMd = 960,
05   limitLg = 1280,
06   loadedSm = false,
07   loadedMd = false,
08   loadedLg = false,
09   loadedXl = false;
10
11 function loadSm() {
12   console.log("load the scripts for small screens");
13 }
```

```
14 function loadMd() {
15   console.log("load the scripts for medium screens");
16 }
17 function loadLg() {
18   console.log("load the scripts for large screens");
19 }
20 function loadXl() {
21   console.log("load scripts for extra large screens");
22 }
23 function logistics() {
24   var cw = document.documentElement.clientWidth;
25   if (cw < limitSm) {
26     if(!loadedSm) {
27       loadSm();
28       loadedSm = true;
29     }
30   } else if (cw < limitMd) {
31     if(!loadedMd){
32       loadMd();
33       loadedMd = true;
34     }
35   } else if (cw < limitLg) {
36     if(!loadedLg){
37       loadLg();
38       loadedLg = true;
39     }
40   } else {
41     if(!loadedXl){
42       loadXl();
43       loadedXl = true;
44     }
45   }
46 };
47 // Screen sized reloading:
48 window.onload = logistics();
49 window.onresize = function(){
50   if (resize != null) {
51     clearTimeout(resize);
52   }
53   resize = setTimeout(function(){
54     console.log("window resized");
55     logistics();
56   }, 750);
57 }
```

If you have a fair amount of JavaScript experience, you should be able to work out what is being accomplished in Listing 12.1. For those without experience, I walk through the listing and explain how it works.

Starting with lines 1–9, several variables are created. These are grouped as Globals because they can be used globally inside other functions in this script.

Lines 11–46 contain functions that will be triggered when the screen size is detected and changes. Some of these functions are called from the `logistics()` function.

Line 48 will run the first time the page is loaded. This calls the `logistics()` function, which then determines the width of the screen and sets it as a variable. You can see the variable being set on line 24; it is then compared to some of the global variables on lines 25, 30, and 35. If it happens to meet any of the conditions on these lines, it will trigger the function inside the `if` statement, and the function contained within will be called.

For example, if `cw` contained a value of `360`, it would meet the condition set on line 25. The first time the condition was met, the variable `loadedSm` would be set to `false`, so the code on lines 27 and 28 would be processed.

Line 27 calls the `loadSm()` function, which is contained on lines 11–13. As shown on line 12, a `console.log()` statement is used that displays a message in your browser console.

Depending on the value of `cw`, different functions are triggered, enabling you to customize the code that is used on your page. By switching the JavaScript `console.log()` statements to `alert()` statements Figure 12.5 demonstrates the message triggering on differently sized screens and devices.

Note that the message windows displayed in Figure 12.5 look slightly different from each other. This is because the message is displayed using the settings and styles determined by the browser.

Depending on your use case, you might want to trigger scripts only once. The variables of `loadedSm`, `loadedMd`, `loadedLg`, and `loadedXl` prevent functions from being called again. By removing these variables, you can run your scripts every time a screen change is detected.

Tip

You might remember when the `alert()` function was widely used during development as a debugging method. This fell by the wayside but lives on today as `console.log()`. This newer replacement offers a wide array of options for testing and monitoring your JavaScript code. Be warned, however, that some browsers (such as Internet Explorer 9 and below) do not handle this function gracefully. Always remove your `console.log()` functions when you are done using them—and definitely before you push the code into production.

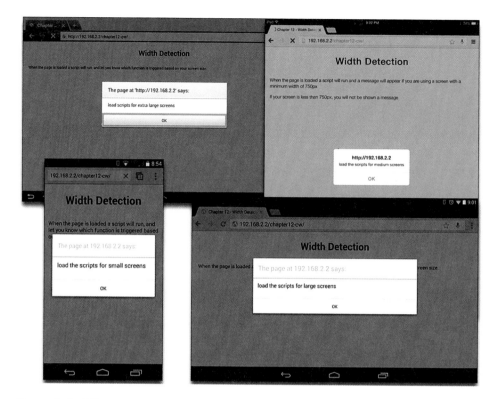

Figure 12.5　Different messages are displayed based on the screen size of the device.

By using this script, you can solve problems such as when to load a carousel, add a plugin, or even programmatically adjust elements to match the space available.

To view this in action, I set up a sample page that you can view on your own device at www.mobiledesignrecipes.com/rmd/chapter12/. This page was developed using the code from Listing 12.1, along with an extra function to load a slider when viewed on a device with a screen that has a minimum width of 768px.

If you use a device that has a small resolution width when held in portrait orientation and a larger one when viewed in landscape orientation, you might notice some interesting effects when changing orientation. If the page is loaded when the device is held in landscape orientation, the slider will be loaded and will stay loaded when the orientation is switched to portrait. This is not true, however, if you start in portrait orientation. In this instance, a single image is displayed first, and then the slider is loaded when switching to landscape orientation. Figure 12.6 demonstrates different devices loading the page.

Note that, in this example, the first image is loaded on larger devices. To fix this, you might want to consider using an element with an intrinsic ratio as a placeholder and then injecting either an image or a slider based on screen size.

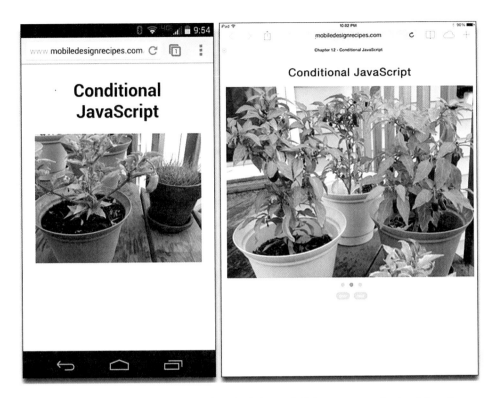

Figure 12.6 Small screens are shown only a single image (left); larger screens load a slider with multiple images (right).

Using JavaScript Plugins

Implementing the script from the previous section might work well for your needs, but sometimes you might find it faster and more efficient to use a script that is already "in the wild." These scripts are commonly referred to as plugins and are available from plugin repositories, code repositories, and even code example sites. Good places to find plugins are GitHub (https://github.com/), Codepen (http://codepen.io/), and the jQuery plugins site (http://plugins.jquery.com/). This is because of the ease of reaching the developer, reading what other users have run into, and having a centralized location to find updates and bug fixes.

jRespond

jRespond (https://github.com/ten1seven/jRespond) has been around for a while and is one of the better choices for managing JavaScript inside responsive and adaptive websites. jRespond was one of the go-to plugins that my team used when we built one of our first fully responsive websites.

To get started with jRespond, you need to include the plugin in your site and then initialize it by adding the breakpoints that you want it to watch for. After that, you define functions that will run on entry into a breakpoint and on exit from that size. An exit occurs when the screen rotates or when the browser screen is resized.

It is a fairly flexible framework that can help you achieve the speed and experience you want your users to have.

mediaCheck

If you visited the jRespond site, you might have noticed a note from the developer that if legacy browser support is not a concern, you should look at mediaCheck (https://github.com/sparkbox/mediaCheck). mediaCheck is brought to you by the amazing Sparkbox team. It works with the `matchMedia()` function with a fallback for window resize events.

The `matchMedia()` function enables you to use information from the browser to see if the current viewable area fits a CSS media query. The following snippet checks whether the current browser would fit a 320px media query. If so, it runs a function:

```
if (window.matchMedia("(min-width: 320px)").matches) {
  alert('Your screen is at least 320px wide!');
}
```

This can be augmented with an `else`, `if else`, or similar logic function to handle multiple media queries. Even though this is JavaScript, for a less "JavaScripty" and more CSS feel, give mediaCheck a look. If you are curious about which browser will be leveraging the fallback support, you can see a list of specific browser support for `matchMedia()` by visiting http://caniuse.com/matchmedia.

ConditionerJS

ConditionerJS (http://conditionerjs.com/) bills itself as "Frizz free, environment aware, JavaScript modules." If your development team is currently using RequireJS (http://requirejs.org/), you would be doing it a favor by introducing ConditionerJS.

As a fair warning, at the time of writing, ConditionerJS is under development. As such, you should treat it as an experimental plugin and use it with care. I mention it here because it is a promising plugin that fits in well with modular architecture.

Covering the usage and setup of ConditionerJS is beyond the scope of this book. The ConditionerJS website provides an abundance of documentation covering setup and usage.

Summary

In this chapter, you learned that conditional JavaScript is not something to ignore. You can use it to help you load the plugins that your page needs at the right time, and it can help you lower the size of your site by not including files that your users will not be using.

You also learned how you can use JavaScript to detect and run functions based on the current screen size. This was accomplished with some example code that can be modified and used on your projects.

Finally, you learned about some plugins that can help you manage your JavaScript based on screen size. You also learned about the `matchMedia` function and a plugin that can help you apply it to your project.

CHAPTER 13

WEB COMPONENTS

Web components are the everyday heroes of the Web. If you have ever created a style guide or worked on a project that repeatedly used elements of your design, you can understand the need for web components. Each repeatable portion of your design has the potential to be used as a web component.

Until recently, it was nearly impossible to create a custom functional component that could be used in a repeatable way. In this chapter, you learn about what makes up a web component and, more importantly, how to create your own that will work right now.

Working with Web Components

You might not realize it, but you already know what a web component is—and you have probably already used them on some of your projects. Developers and designers use web components every day on various web projects to add widgets and extra functionality to a website or application.

The best way to get started with web components is to view some examples that you might already be familiar with. Then I walk you through the Document Object Model (DOM) and the Shadow DOM. To finish, I show you some polyfill projects that you can leverage now that enable you to use your own custom web components instead of having to wait for baked-in browser support.

> ## Tip
>
> You might be unsure of what a polyfill is. Remy Sharp defines it as follows: "A polyfill, or polyfiller, is a piece of code (or plugin) that provides the technology that you, the developer, expect the browser to provide natively" (http://remysharp.com/2010/10/08/what-is-a-polyfill/). Some plugins use polyfills so that every browser gets a very similar, if not identical, experience.

Examples of Web Components

A web component is made up of several elements that then have specific functionality and are tied together with various styles and JavaScript to make them work.

You can think of a web component as a specialized widget that you will be using for a specific purpose either multiple times or in multiple places on your site.

Audio Element

The HTML `audio` element is an excellent example of a web component. The following code is an example of how to use the `audio` element in your HTML file:

```
<audio controls>
  <source src="audio.ogg" type="audio/ogg">
  <source src="audio.mp3" type="audio/mpeg">
  This browser does not support the audio element
</audio>
```

When this code is rendered in a browser, it displays an object that looks nothing like the HTML markup that was used. Figure 13.1 demonstrates the `audio` element viewed in a browser.

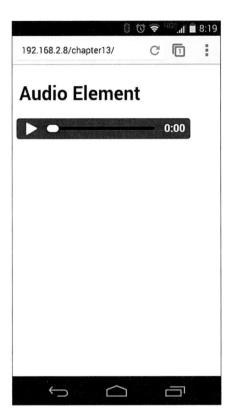

Figure 13.1 An audio player is displayed with a Play/Pause button, a scrubber, a duration button, and volume control.

This simple audio player is rather amazing. It contains elements and functionality that are already available to you without having to add any styles or JavaScript. In fact, if you were to look at the code that goes into making the player, you would find that the audio player is put together with several `div` and `input` elements.

The browser then styles these elements in what is called the user-agent stylesheet. Every browser ships with a version of this stylesheet and uses it to render default elements. This is one of the reasons some developers and designers use a reset stylesheet: It specifically sets the styles for a multitude of elements, which forces the browser to discard the built-in styles and use the reset ones.

Now take a look at another example of a web component that is already in use: the `video` element.

Video Element

The `video` element is closely related to the `audio` element, and with good reason. Both are used for the playback of media files. The main difference, of course, is that the `video` element plays back video files instead of just audio tracks.

You can use the following `video` element markup in your HTML to display a video:

```
<video controls>
  <source src="video.mp4" type="video/mp4">
  <source src="video.ogg" type="video/ogg">
  This browser does not support the video element
</video>
```

Depending on the browser you are using, a player that is similar to the one rendered for audio tracks will appear. Figure 13.2 shows the `video` element rendered in a browser.

Figure 13.2   An area for the video is shown, along with some familiar controls to manipulate video playback.

As Figure 13.2 shows, the `video` element has been transformed into a collection of elements that are then wired together and styled by the browser.

It might help you to think about this like a common object. You probably know what a bicycle looks like, and you know that even when it appears in a different configuration (say, a road bike compared to a mountain bike), it is still a bicycle. As with an actual bicycle, you can swap out components and create a customized experience by using web components. In this manner, you create an object that will appear the same in every browser.

The last example of web components that are currently in use is a type of `input`.

Date Input

If you have ever worked on an application or site that required a user to schedule a date, enter a date, or otherwise use a date, you might have used an `input` with a type of `date`.

The HTML markup for using this type of input is as easy as using the following snippet:

```
<input type="date" name="myDate" id="myDate">
```

This particular `input` is actually more than a little interesting because of how it renders on various browsers and devices. Chrome renders this input as a web component that includes multiple control options. This makes it extremely convenient for users to enter dates and see how the date should be formatted to reduce user error.

Other browsers, however, do not have a web component built in for this particular type of element and instead display an `input` element with a type of `text`. Figure 13.3 demonstrates how this input type is rendered on various browsers.

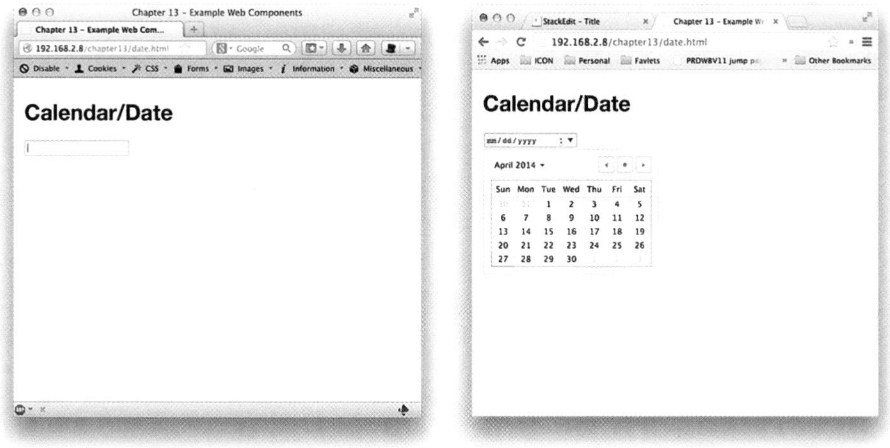

Figure 13.3   Firefox (left) displays a rather stark text input field, whereas Chrome (right) displays a fully functioning calendar widget.

Without knowing that browsers display this element differently, you would be in for an extreme amount of code refactoring and a visual overhaul of the user experience when moving your code into a staging or production environment.

This is one of the main reasons you should perform testing on as many systems and browsers as possible before sending your code out to a production server.

Another reason I wanted you to view this example was so you could see that relying on browser-styled elements is not a good idea unless you can guarantee that 100% of your users will be using that rendering engine.

To start using your own web components that will work cross-browser, you first need to learn about the DOM and the Shadow DOM.

Working with the DOM

The DOM is a model that is used to turn elements into objects. You can think of it as a way for browsers and similar programs to organize HTML and XML elements. JavaScript developers also can leverage it as an API.

Web browsers use the DOM to parse HTML elements and create what is called the DOM tree. This is then used to render your code, along with your styles and JavaScript, into the page that you can see on your screen.

The DOM has a fairly rich history and is still being improved and modified. Currently, DOM Level 3 is the standard, but DOM Level 4 is being finalized and will become the new standard shortly.

As mentioned earlier, the DOM is also an API that can be used to locate specific elements and enable you to manipulate or use data from them.

The following is an example of how the DOM can be accessed in JavaScript:

```
document.getElementById("container");
```

In this code snippet, the DOM tree is accessed with the use of `document`. Then to select the element that contains an ID of `container`, the method `getElementById()` is used with a value of `container`.

Running this script returns the element from the DOM tree that matches these criteria. The returned object also includes any child elements. Figure 13.4 shows the result of running this script on a sample page.

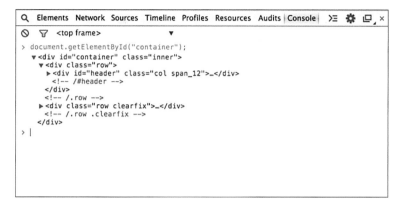

Figure 13.4   The command is run from Developer Tools inside Chrome, and the returned object is expanded to show child elements.

As Figure 13.4 shows, the returned elements contain the HTML (including comments) that was used to build the web page. These elements are all taken from the DOM tree and should look familiar.

By modifying the JavaScript snippet and using the console of Chrome Developer Tools, or Firefox with Firebug or the Web Console, you can select other elements on your page and view the returned data. All this data is part of the standard DOM tree, but how does this help with creating web components? I'm glad you asked; let me give you a peek at the Shadow DOM.

The Shadow DOM

If you have ever tried to create a widget or a JavaScript plugin, you might have encountered the problem of duplicate IDs.

This happened to me once when I created a modal plugin that displayed specific content while changing the opacity of the background elements so that users would focus on what I wanted them to see. The problem was that my plugin was using common names for various IDs, such as `content`, `field`, and `container`.

When duplicate IDs are used in HTML, your JavaScript and styles will not behave the way you expect. This results in bugs that are difficult to fix and widespread chaos in your design. In the end, I had to prefix every class and ID my plugin used, to avoid running into duplicates. However, this exact issue is part of what makes the Shadow DOM so appealing.

When using the Shadow DOM, you no longer need to worry about duplicate IDs or classes. Each element in the Shadow DOM is not part of the global DOM tree. This gives you the capability to create elements that have names that make sense semantically and that can be self-contained.

You might be thinking that you can already create widgets, plugins, and more by using other elements, such as `canvas`. True, many applications—even games—are built using the wonderfully compatible `canvas` element. However, as Dominic Cooney points out on the HTML5Rocks website, "it's hostile to accessibility, indexing, composition, and resolution independence." Now that you know why you should be using the Shadow DOM, let me show you how it is used.

Using a Template

To be completely fair, you do not actually have to use the `template` element. You have other ways and methods (such as using `.innerHTML`) to create Shadow DOM elements. However, the `template` element is currently supported by many modern browsers including Firefox, Chrome, and Opera (see http://caniuse.com/template for the current list of supported browsers). Because of this, and because it plays very well with polyfill projects such as Polymer, I show you how to create Shadow DOM elements using the `template` element.

Using the `template` element, you can create the styles and structure used for a web component. The following is a skeleton that can be fleshed out for creating a web component:

```
<template id="myElementTemplate">
  <style>
    /* style me up */
  </style>
  <div>
    structure elements go here
  </div>
</template>
```

The `template` elements that you create will not be rendered when the page loads. Loading the elements from the template requires you to create a copy of the template code and insert it into the DOM tree.

To do that, you need to use JavaScript to select an element to populate and a template to use for population. The following snippet shows how this is accomplished:

```
<script>
  var shadow = document.querySelector('#item').createShadowRoot();
  var template = document.querySelector('#itemTemplate');
  shadow.appendChild(template.content);
  template.remove();
</script>
```

Tip

Not all browsers natively support the JavaScript functions needed to work with the Shadow DOM. For the examples in this book, Chrome Canary was used because it supports Shadow DOM manipulation.

The widget or component that you are adding might be completely self-contained and ready to be added to the page. However, if you have data that needs to be dynamic, you have to use the content element.

Editing Content

The content element works inside your template, to allow you to alter the data of your component. It also gives you the capability to manipulate the data with JavaScript.

Using the skeleton template shown previously, you can create a button and add a content element to change the text of the button.

```
<template id="myButtonTemplate">
  <style>
    /* style me up */
  </style>
  <div class="container">
    <div class="inner">
      <content></content>
    </div>
  </div>
</template>
```

Now that you have a content element inside the template element, by using some JavaScript, you can change the value of the button with the following snippet of code:

```
document.querySelector('#myButton').textContent = 'Unto Dawn!';
```

Note that the value passed in the querySelector is not #myButtonTemplate, but another element with an ID of myButton. To be more specific, the value used in this querySelector statement should be the one you used when you created the shadow root by using the createShadowRoot() method. In the code snippet, document is used to access the DOM. The querySelect() method finds the element with an ID of myButton. textContent gets the value of the content element, which is then set to contain a value of "Unto Dawn!".

The Shadow DOM is an exciting part of web technology right now, and you should do as much as you can to be informed about using it and learn how it will help you shape not only your design, but the entire structure of code that supports it. This has been an introduction to how to get started with it, but you can use other resources to push the limits of content delivery.

To learn more about the Shadow DOM and how to use it, visit the following resources:

- www.html5rocks.com/en/tutorials/webcomponents/shadowdom/
- www.html5rocks.com/en/tutorials/webcomponents/shadowdom-201/
- www.html5rocks.com/en/tutorials/webcomponents/shadowdom-301/
- www.w3.org/TR/components-intro/#shadow-dom-section

Web Component Polyfills

As mentioned earlier, not every browser currently supports the functions needed to fully implement the various aspects and elements that make up web components. This is where polyfills come to the rescue.

A polyfill is code that fills in the gaps that are missing in a browser supporting a particular piece of code.

In the past, a popular polyfill has been respond.js. This polyfill adds CSS3 media query support to the Internet Explorer 6, 7, and 8 web browsers. Using respond.js was critical to early responsive web development because many users were either unable or unaware of the availability of alternate web browsers that provided a more modern web experience.

When it comes to supporting web components, you can use a couple of polyfill libraries right now to get started in the right direction.

Polymer

The first time I heard about the Polymer project (http://www.polymer-project.org/) was when Eric Bidelman (who works for Google as a Senior Developer Programs Engineer) gave a fantastic presentation titled "Web Components: A Tectonic Shift for Web Development" at Google I/O in May 2013. I heard his presentation again at the Breaking Development Conference a couple months later. Both times Eric presented, he mesmerized the audience with masterful control of fully customizable widgets and objects that could be easily replicated and used.

Aside from the easy-to-extend functionality of the platform, what makes Polymer so attractive is that it enables you to develop your code using the emerging standard for web components. Even if you are worried about compatibility or cross-browser functionality, Polymer uses myriad polyfills to handle, or at least gracefully degrade, most (if not all) modern browsers

This means that if a browser doesn't currently support the Shadow DOM, the Polymer library will implement a scripted version of it. This gives you a shot at having clean code that will run natively (pending browser support) but has graceful degradation built in.

Polymer Elements

The team that works on Polymer has done some truly amazing work. Furthermore, the team has realized that many of the elements it is using are ones it would like to use in multiple projects.

By leveraging the Bower (http://bower.io/) package manager, the elements the team has built and continues to use (not to mention update) are available for you to pull into your project.

If you already have Bower installed on your system and have included Polymer in your web project, you can easily add specific Polymer elements from the command line.

For example, if you wanted to add flexbox to your layout, you would want to include the `core-layout` element. To add this using Bower, you would type the following into your terminal:

```
bower install --save Polymer/core-layout
```

Bower is an awesome package manager for development because it keeps your repositories up-to-date. This helps you develop with the latest stable code. In fact, the previous snippet that uses Bower actually references the GitHub location https://github.com/Polymer/core-layout, where the core layout code is maintained.

To learn about the available elements and see the list of currently available ones, visit http://polymer.github.io/core-docs/components/core-docs/.

The Polymer project provides an exciting opportunity for both design and development with flexibility, control, and reusable components.

X-Tag

Another way you can get started using web components right now is to leverage the Mozilla X-Tag project (http://www.x-tags.org/). The X-Tag project has excellent browser support and currently works with the following:

- Firefox 5+
- Chrome 4+
- Android 2.1+
- Safari 4+
- Internet Explorer 9+
- Opera 11+

One major difference that you will find when using X-Tag versus Polymer is that it does not offer a polyfill for working with the Shadow DOM. The X-Tag team decided that, instead of solving possible performance problems when working with the Shadow DOM (or creating a pseudo one), the team would focus on other ways to work with custom elements and components.

X-Tag works by using JavaScript to register an element with the DOM and then using several methods to perform extra processing or work as the element is added to and rendered on the DOM. For a detailed guide of the process, be sure to visit the documentation section of the X-Tag website (http://www.x-tags.org/docs). It has an example of registering a component and walks through all the available methods to make it work.

Although you can use jQuery, Dojo, and other JavaScript libraries on your web page, when using X-Tag, there is no requirement for any of these. You can use the standard DOM API calls to get your entire web component setup done so that your site contains less code and more speed.

If you have consulted the documentation and are a little overwhelmed, fear not: You can always check out a component library called Brick.

Using Brick

Brick (http://mozilla.github.io/brick/) is an aptly named project because it contains many web components, or bricks, that can help you prototype, build, and even wrap your head around the potential power of using web components.

Brick is currently divided into the following ready-to-use components:

- `calendar`
- `flipbox`
- `slider`
- `toggle`
- `appbar`
- `deck`
- `layout`
- `tabbar`

When you decide that you would like to download and get started using Brick, to help you optimize your file size, you can choose which components to include. You then need to include the downloaded CSS and JavaScript file in your HTML.

It is also worth noting that the components of Brick are available for use in Bower. To see the documentation on using the components, as well as how to include them in your web projects with Bower, view the official documentation at http://mozilla.github.io/brick/docs.html.

Summary

This chapter introduced you to web components and why you want to use them. You saw some web components that you might already be using today, as well as some that do not work with all browsers.

You then learned about the DOM, including the Shadow DOM. You saw that the Shadow DOM is a way to render elements that live outside the global scope of the DOM tree onto the page.

You also discovered some polyfill projects that you can use right now to create your own web components, as well as use prebuilt elements.

CHAPTER 14

DEVICE DETECTION AND SERVER REQUESTS

This chapter covers the current solutions for device detection and the process to follow when a browser requests resources from a server.

Having a server that can understand the capabilities of the device is beneficial for both the user and the developer. By knowing what to serve, you can send the right file, at the right size, and keep your HTML markup clean and neat. This helps you keep your site manageable and your visitors happy.

Device Detection

During the course of your job, you will at some point be required to create, design, or build a product that must work for myriad users. In some cases, this will be a relatively easy task: The parameters of the projects will be laid out quite neatly, and you will simply fulfill them.

Other times, your employer will require you to create a specific experience for a subset of devices. This is when you will need to use some form of device detection.

Regardless of why you would need to serve different content to a different device, you have a few ways to get this done. The following lists the common methods in use for detecting various devices:

- Using JavaScript detection
- Reading the user-agent string
- Implementing a device database

Each of these methods works. However, each also comes with some caveats that you should be aware of before diving in.

Using JavaScript Detection

You can use JavaScript to perform a series of tests and then invoke various polyfills, add or remove CSS imports, or perform redirects based on the device detected.

> **Tip**
>
> Using JavaScript for device detection can be useful for setting various portions of your site or to progressively enhance your site based on the device viewing it. It is not generally a good method for mobile site redirection.

The key to using JavaScript for device detection is to make sure that the script is executed first. This can be done by leveraging the `onload` event. As an example, you can use the following HTML skeleton:

```
<!DOCTYPE html>
<html>
  <head>
    <script>
      window.onload = function() {
        // Your JavaScript detection code goes here
      }
    </script>
```

```
    <title>My Site</title>
  </head>
  <body>
    <!-- Site code goes here -->
  </body>
</html>
```

This code should appear to be completely backward from everything you have already learned about JavaScript placement. JavaScript is code that "blocks" the browser from further rendering or processing until it has completed the code inside the `<script>` element. By placing the code immediately inside the `<head>` element, you guarantee that it will "block" the browser from containing and that the script will run.

The first line of the JavaScript is `window.onload`, which makes the code execute during the loading process of the page. The JavaScript that you want to execute needs to be added in place of the comment `Your JavaScript detection code goes here`.

The code you choose to run will vary based on what you would like to accomplish. Some services use code in this way to attach A/B tests, use redirects, and even use a regex to determine the device being used so that different styles, scripts, and widgets will be loaded for the appropriate device.

Figure 14.1 demonstrates this code that uses the `alert()` function to halt page processing.

The following is a list of pros and cons when using JavaScript as a device detection method:

Pros:

- Easy to implement
- Enables you to change site settings based on the device detected
- Works with hosting providers that do not give you access to your server configuration, such as shared hosting or shared virtual server providers

Cons:

- Stops your page from rendering while your logic is executed
- Gives users who are redirected a white screen before being magically redirected
- Offers a client-side solution that could be more elegantly handled on the server
- Impacts the loading time your users experience

Figure 14.1   The devices are detected and information is displayed on screen.

Reading the User-Agent String

A few years ago, I was asked to create a mobile site for a large eCommerce client. One of the main requirements was that all "mobile" devices were to be redirected to the "mobile" version of the site that was hosted at a different domain.

> **Tip**
>
> Hosting separate domains for your content is a strategy you should thoroughly think through before committing to it. Many search providers will punish your search ranking for hosting the same site on different domains because of duplicate content and a less-than-stellar user experience. By the same token, if you use canonical URLs and other meta information, hosting a separate site might work in your favor.

The idea behind this particular task was that devices would first pull up the standard www.domain.com site, and then the server would query the device "type" and "mobile" users would be redirected to the m.domain.com site. Figure 14.2 demonstrates the request flow.

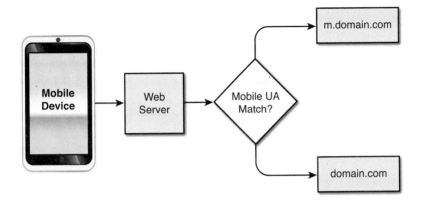

Figure 14.2 Depending on the device making the request, the device can be routed to a different domain.

The device detection was done through a very simple query that involves the user-agent string. The user-agent (UA) string is a short bit of information available from the browser making requests that helps identify what the device is capable of and has some unique features.

A sample UA string follows:

```
Mozilla/5.0 (Linux; U; Android 2.3.4; en-us; Kindle Fire HD Build/GINGERBREAD)
AppleWebKit/533.1 (KHTML, like Gecko) Version/4.0 Mobile Safari/533.1
```

Knowing that most mobile devices will identify themselves in such a way that they are grouped as mobile, I only needed to write a query on the web server that would look at the request and redirect the device if needed.

By using a mod rewrite (http://httpd.apache.org/docs/current/mod/mod_rewrite.html) on my Apache server, I added the following to my `httpd.conf` file:

```
RewriteCond %{HTTP_USER_AGENT} "android|blackberry|iphone|ipod|
➥iemobile|opera mobile|palmos|webos|googlebot-mobile" [NC]
```

This particular rewrite creates a test condition that uses the `HTTP_USER_AGENT`, which contains the UA string. If it finds any of the strings in the list, the condition returns `true` and further processing (such as a redirect) can be done on the server.

The following is a list of pros and cons for this particular method:

Pros:

- Easy to implement
- Can be adjusted to drop certain devices
- Can use a cookie to bypass the routing

Cons:

- Requires maintaining the list, to accommodate new devices and user agents
- Forces some devices, such as tablets, to go to the mobile site even when they are not "mobile" device tablets
- Evaluates every request if this is used in an `.htaccess` file
- Accepts that not all devices will be specific when it comes to self-identification
- Potentially involves duplicate content from search engines and a penalty for multiple sites

Choosing to use the UA string for device grouping can be a relatively fast solution, but the potential damage to your search engine marketing/optimization might not be worth the risk. Using canonical URLs might mitigate some risk, but this introduces new complications with dynamic pages. Other problems, such as serving mobile versions of the site to large-screen tablets such as iPads, can cause user headache.

To reiterate, this is a solution that you can set up quickly, but unless you are able to keep up with the potential maintenance, it is not a viable long-term solution.

Implementing a Device Database

A different take on using a UA string for device detection is to use a list or database of devices. Most of these databases contain lists of specific device information that an application or server can use to identify and group devices based on the characteristics of that device.

The databases depend on using portions of the UA string, screen size, pixel density, and various hardware features. As a device requests a page from your server, the server queries the device and then checks the list to see what type of device it is so that it can either send it the correct information or page or redirect it to another page or site.

One of the most common and longest-running device databases is the Wireless Universal Resource File (WURFL). WURFL (www.scientiamobile.com/) is available in a few different versions and for different web servers. For example, an API can be accessed to help identify devices, and a server plugin can be used in place of the API calls. Note that some of the services available from WURFL are commercial and must be purchased.

An open-source alternative to WURFL is the Open Device Description Repository (OpenDDR). OpenDDR (www.openddr.org/) offers API calls and device listings and is available for Java and .NET users.

The following is a list of pros and cons when using a device database for device detection:

Pros:

- Most devices will be detected, allowing you to handle them.
- Both free and commercial options are available.
- Some content delivery networks offer this solution as part of the hosting cost.
- Content can be tailored per device.

Cons:

- The list must be maintained in a market that has new devices released monthly, in similar fashion to the user agent list.
- For best results, the solution must be integrated on a server level, which requires extra setup and maintenance.
- Updates must be either purchased or implemented by yourself or the community.
- Not all devices are detectable.

Even though you might want to use a device database for serving content, a few third-party diagnostic applications use a device list like this to help re-create customer experiences. Other platforms and solutions also require a device database to properly serve dynamic files and templates.

Using a device database for mobile identification could be the best solution for you and your server configuration.

HTTP Headers

Device detection can be a required portion of your design and development, but it definitely has limits. So far, you have seen that detection is possible, but it is often a complicated process that does not adequately handle the situation for all devices without some augmentation.

In our search to create "one web" that works on every device, we need to get down to the nuts and bolts of how web browsers work. Before you start to feel ether seep out of these pages, let me assure you that I am not going to give you a discourse on C and teach you to build your own HTML parsing engine. What I will teach you is how requests are made between the server and your browser.

To get started, the following is the simplified version of a user getting a web page:

1. The user enters a URL into the browser.
2. The browser performs a DNS lookup to find the server.
3. The server replies with a status message and, hopefully, the requested site.
4. The browser renders the server response to the user.

You might not realize it, but portions of this model are repeated for every asset on a website. This includes images, styles, JavaScript files, and all other site assets.

Another portion of this process that I am sure you are already familiar with is the status messages. The following is a list of the status ranges:

- **100s:** Informational
- **200s:** Successful
- **300s:** Redirects
- **400s:** Client errors
- **500s:** Server errors

Seeing this list, you might recognize that files you request that return with a status message of 200 mean that the request was successful.

Seeing a 301 or a 302 message means that the item you have requested has been moved, and a 304 means that the file you want is already in your browser cache.

A status message of 403 means that you do not have access to the file, folder, or asset you are requesting. This is similar to the 404 message, which means the item you requested cannot be located, or is "Not Found."

A flat 500 status message means that the server is having difficulty processing or connecting to another part of the system. These errors are typically seen during system outages and upgrades.

To continue the dive into HTTP requests, when a request is made from your browser, it sends what is called a request header and receives back a response header. Figure 14.3 shows a request made for an HTML file.

As Figure 14.3 shows, the file returned with a status of 200, letting you know that the page request was successful. You can also see that the user-agent was passed to the server, and you can see the UA string, as well as the browser informing the server that the Do Not Track (DNT) flag was turned on.

Figure 14.3 The browser sends information about what it is capable of processing, and the server sends back information that the browser will use to process content.

For the response, you can see that the server is returning the file with `gzip` compression and that the response contains a MIME type of text/html. Letting the browser know that the file is compressed and should be parsed and displayed as HTML is crucial to rendering the site properly.

Other bits of information from both the request (client) and the response (server) are useful when you are fine-tuning your server. To learn more about what they mean, visit https://developer.mozilla.org/en-US/docs/Web/HTTP and http://en.wikipedia.org/wiki/List_of_HTTP_header_fields.

Using Client Hints

Detecting the device that is viewing your site is helpful for making decisions and for changing content. However, many of the discussed methods require a form of sniffing, scanning, or even delaying the page load to make changes.

Another interesting detail is that every HTTP request sent to a server contains information about the device making the request. If we could use this method to identify key features of a device and then cater content to it, we would have a serious time saver that would get us closer to providing a better experience to the user.

It turns out that a new potential specification is being championed by Ilya Grigorik, web performance engineer and developer advocate at Google. This specification is called Client Hints.

In the current proposal, Client Hints provides the following information from the browser to the server:

- **CH-DPR:** Device Pixel Ratio
- **CH-RW:** Resource Width, given in device-independent pixels

You might not realize it, but having these values gives you some fairly impressive capabilities. Knowing the actual dimensions of a device without relying on JavaScript guesswork can help you get correct analytics for users visiting your site. JavaScript depends on what the browser returns as a value. Many times, this information can be incorrect: The window of the browser and even the screen pixel density can throw off calculations. This, in turn, enables you to fine-tune your design and create an experience that meets the needs of your users.

By throwing in the pixel ratio of the device, you can set up the server to serve images or assets from a different location than the default. You might be wondering why that is helpful, so let me show you why this is an exciting feature.

If you have an image that needs to be shown at Retina resolution when a device requests it, you could use the following markup:

```
<img alt="detailed feature"
    src="detail1x.jpg"
    srcset="detail1x.jpg 1x, detail2x.jpg 2x, detail3x.jpg 3x">
```

Before you get excited and slap this code into your page, note that this markup relies on `srcset` working in your browser.

By using `srcset`, the correct image is served based on the capabilities of the device. This means that most iPhones will request the `detail2x.jpg` image, whereas Samsung Galaxy phones will tend to request and use the `detail3x.jpg` image.

And now for a little magic: By using Client Hints and a little server configuration adjustment, you can use the following code to serve the correct image to a user:

```
<img alt="detailed feature" src="detail.jpg">
```

I will give you a minute to adjust your jaw. Yes, that really is the only markup needed. Let me break down how the magic happens.

An iPhone makes a request to the server and passes the following information as part of the request header:

```
GET /detail.jpg HTTP/1.1
User-Agent: Mozilla/5.0 (iPhone; CPU iPhone OS 7_0 like Mac OS X; en-us)
AppleWebKit/537.51.1 (KHTML, like Gecko) Version/7.0 Mobile/11A465
Safari/9537.53
Accept: text/html,application/xhtml+xml,application/xml;q=0.9,image/
webp,*/*;q=0.8
CH-DPR: 2.0
CH-RW: 320
```

The server (which has been configured to use and support Client Hints) looks at the `CH-DPR` and `CH-RW` values. It performs the following calculation:

```
CH-RW * CH-DPR = requiredWidth
```

In the case of the example, the iPhone request will be read as:

```
320 * 2 = 640
```

This can then be appended to the image request so that a file named `detail640.jpg` will be served to the user.

This does require some work, but with multiple server-side image processing options available, you could provide a few images and then let images be created and cached as needed.

Client Hints is an emerging technology and is still being finalized. You can learn more, submit ideas, and keep up with the development by visiting the following links:

- https://github.com/igrigorik/http-client-hints
- http://tools.ietf.org/html/draft-grigorik-http-client-hints-01
- www.igvita.com/2013/08/29/automating-dpr-switching-with-client-hints/

Summary

In this chapter, you learned about detecting devices by using JavaScript, the user-agent string, and a device database.

You also learned about HTTP requests and responses. This included the definition of various status codes and how browsers give servers information about what they are capable of using.

Finally, you learned about an emerging future technology called Client Hints that aims to keep code clean and automate asset delivery.

CHAPTER 15

SERVER OPTIMIZATION

Crafting the perfect mobile experience doesn't end with curated content and a design that morphs to fit the screen viewing it. The actual delivery of your design is paramount for increased transactions, user happiness, and recommendations. Unfortunately, you cannot do much to control the actual speed of a user's connection; however, you can make sure that your server is pushing the right content in the fastest way possible.

In this chapter, you learn about web servers, what they are capable of serving, and the plugins you can use to optimize them for peak performance.

Server Setup

Optimizing your server for the best possible delivery varies based on the type of server you decide to use. This particular topic itself is worthy of a book covering the entire process of installation, management, and setup. This chapter lists popular servers, where you can get them, and some information about what they can do.

I also list some modules and plugins that can maximize your content delivery. These plugins are not for every server. However, the reasoning behind using them, as well as what they do, should give you a working knowledge of the important considerations when setting up a server and finding or creating other plugins for your own setup.

Web Servers

Cracking open an HTML template and the accompanying styles for a quick edit might work for a quick prototype. Even using various site-generation tools, such as Adobe Reflow and Edge, can create fully functional HTML, CSS, and JavaScript files that can be passed to developers for site implementation.

You might not realize, though, that many different types of web servers are available, and each works differently. That is not to say that they are all completely different, but when you start out with a prototype HTML project, it could very well end up as an ASP, JSP, PHP, or other file type and project.

Apache

The Apache HTTP web server (http://httpd.apache.org/) has long been the trusted sidekick, if not beleaguered champion, of all things web related. The Apache server turned 17 in February 2014, proving that it has been time and battle tested as the sole provider, cluster member, and file server.

With excellent support for serving files, generally all that is needed to serve a new file type is to add the Multipurpose Internet Mail Extensions (MIME) type to the server configuration file. It also includes the capability to be extended through web modules. The general rule for modules is that, if you have a need for it, there is a good chance that someone else built a module for it.

Another benefit of this server is that it has been around long enough that it is included by default in almost every Linux build and application repository. This makes it easy to create your own "cloud" server or Virtual Private Server (VPS) and get it up and running.

Nginx

Nginx (pronounced "engine-ex") is another web server that shares some similarities with the Apache web server. It can be used as a "standard" web server for serving content and data, and it can also be configured as a reverse proxy for other systems, including email (POP, SMTP, and IMAP) and content caching (HTTP and HTTPS).

The Nginx server has a different logic model when compared to Apache. Instead of spinning up new threads and using a process-driven approach to handle requests, Nginx works by handling requests in an asynchronous manner. This allows the server to handle a larger load without consuming extra resources.

Dreamhost, a web-hosting and domain name registrar, performed a test comparing Apache, Nginx, and Lighttpd (http://wiki.dreamhost.com/Web_Server_Performance_Comparison). In the testing, it found that Nginx had the smallest memory footprint and had a peak of handling more than 12,000 concurrent connections.

For this reason, Nginx is a popular choice for high-traffic, high-demand websites. To learn more about Nginx, including how to install, configure, and use modules, visit the wiki (http://wiki.nginx.org/).

IIS

If you are looking to serve more than static HTML files and you are running Windows servers, look no further than the IIS server.

At one time, this server was the server that came with the Windows OS. It was installable through the Add/Remove Components section of the Control Panel and was called Internet Information Server.

As the Windows operating system progressed, the name changed to IIS; with the release of each new Windows OS version, a new version of IIS was prepared and shipped.

The IIS server can serve as an HTTP, HTTPS, FTP, FTPS, SMTP, and NNTP server. It can also serve dynamic content because of its support for Active Server Pages (ASP) files.

ASP files allow the use of .NET to create rich, dynamic content that can connect to myriad other systems, including Microsoft SQL, to pull dynamic content that can be part of a content management system.

If you would like to use IIS, you can find hosting providers that offer shared hosting, as well as those that allow you to transfer your Windows licenses to virtual machines, to grant you access to hardware that you might not have otherwise.

IIS can use plugins that extend built-in functionality. Some third-party plugins allow the use of different databases, file types, and, more importantly, thread handling. Learn more about IIS by visiting www.iis.net/.

Tomcat

For Java developers looking to create and serve dynamic websites, the Tomcat server delivers both a local development solution and a robust server that can be used to serve applications to the web.

Tomcat uses applications that are packaged into WAR files that contain all the code (including Java logic and static assets such as CSS and JavaScript) for your site and "deploys" them to the server for user access.

By using JavaServer Page (JSP) files, Java code can be invoked through the use of "beans," as well as discretely embedded as scriptlet code.

Each version of Tomcat released supports a different version of the Java languages. For example, to support Java 7 and up, you need Tomcat 8; to support Java 6, you need to run Tomcat 7.

Tomcat is part of the Apache Foundation and can be downloaded for free at http://tomcat.apache.org/. Support is provided online, but you might find it best to look up a distributor who sells integration and support. This is especially the case when working with advanced concepts such as clustering Tomcat servers.

NodeJS

As a relative newcomer to the web serving game, NodeJS brings the concept of using a client-side language (JavaScript) to create a versatile platform that leverages the V8 processing engine to create a very fast and nimble processing machine.

NodeJS is an asynchronous server (somewhat similar to Nginx) and allows the system to be scaled and replicated on the fly. This is one of the reasons NodeJS is a very popular server for large-scale applications that ebb and flow with users at various points of the day or year.

NodeJS is part of Joyent and is a very active and well-maintained project. Developers love the speed of integration and the capability to leverage front-end skills into a back-end processing environment.

NodeJS has many exceptional plugins, most notable being NPM. NPM is the official package manager for NodeJS, and developers can create and submit packages to the repository for other developers to install and use.

NodeJS runs on Windows, OS X, and Linux systems. You can learn more about using and installing NodeJS at http://nodejs.org/.

Server Plugins

The problem web servers run into fairly often is that they cannot keep up with the surge of technology without suffering either scope creep or feature bloat. Another problem with attempting to always provide cutting-edge technology is that patches have to be pushed often and testing probably suffers.

The solution to this problem is to offer a solid solution that is stable and easy to install. This gives you a standard that you can feel comfortable using and that you know will work for most devices.

New features such as supporting new file types, enabling on-the-fly image processing, and adding file compression can then be gained through the use of server modules or plugins.

Using the correct plugins on your server not only helps you serve new content, but it also allows you to use newer technologies and serve content in an optimized fashion.

Four plugins that you should be considering now with your web server are SPDY, Caching, Reverse Proxy, and Pagespeed.

SPDY

The SPDY protocol came about as part of a Google initiative to deliver web content to users faster than transitional HTTP transmissions allow. At the 2014 Google I/O, Google announced that the SPDY project had become part of the Apache Foundation. As it was originally a Google project, it is almost a given that it works with Chrome; implementations of SPDY also are available for Mozilla Firefox, Opera, Amazon Silk browser, and even Internet Explorer 11.

In keeping with the goal of speeding up web delivery, the HTTP portion of data transmission itself is not changed; instead, the way the data is organized and prioritized is modified for efficiency.

Consider, for example, an HTTPS transmission. Figure 15.1 shows a performance summary of connections to a website using a secure (HTTPS) connection.

Requests made are wrapped up in a layer and negotiated from the server, so the time it takes to deliver assets starts to increase. This reduces the efficiency of the server and slows the page load. Worse, this demonstrates that, without SPDY, secure sites are slower on payload delivery than nonsecure sites.

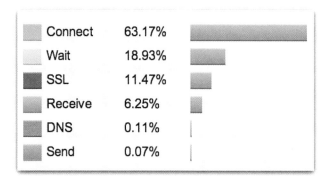

Connect	63.17%	
Wait	18.93%	
SSL	11.47%	
Receive	6.25%	
DNS	0.11%	
Send	0.07%	

Figure 15.1   A report generated from Pingdom Tools shows that SSL is using 11.47% of load time.

The SPDY protocol takes care of the request speed problem by ensuring that the entire payload, not just a single request, is negotiated through a virtual tunnel where requests are threaded, multiplexed, and delivered.

To simplify, all requests for a page, regardless of HTTP or HTTPS, are combined into a single and compressed response.

Using SPDY with Apache

To use SPDY with the Apache 2.2 web server, you need to download the module, which is named mod_spdy (https://developers.google.com/speed/spdy/mod_spdy/). The module can be downloaded as a .deb file for Debian or Ubuntu users or an .rpm file for CentOS and Fedora users. Of course, if you want to get elbows deep into the code, you can always grab the source code and build it yourself.

If you were using an Ubuntu server, you would use the following commands in your terminal to install mod_spdy:

```
sudo dpkg -i mod-spdy-*.deb
sudo apt-get -f install
```

> **Tip**
>
> When using SPDY on Apache, mod_spdy must be served over HTTPS. This means that you need to have a certificate for your site and also have the proper configuration to serve files securely. Note that you do not have to include the mod_ssl when using mod_spdy because a version that includes support for Next Protocol Negotiation (NPN) will be installed with mod_spdy.

After you have installed `mod_spdy`, you need to restart your Apache server. To restart the service, you should be able to use the following:

```
sudo /etc/init.d/apache2 restart
```

If your system uses services or upstart, you need to use the following:

```
sudo service apache2 restart
```

When your server restarts, SPDY should be enabled and running. You can test it by following the instructions at https://developers.google.com/speed/spdy/mod_spdy/.

Using SPDY with Nginx

The Nginx server has supported SPDY since version 1.4.0. This means that not only does SPDY work well with Nginx, but the process of installation is widely documented.

Unfortunately, SPDY cannot be simply dropped into Nginx as a plugin or `mod` file; it must be compiled into your Nginx installation. However, as luck would have it, many Linux repositories already have SPDY compiled into their distributions. To find out if you have support for SPDY baked into your Nginx install, run the following from the terminal:

```
nginx -V
```

This displays a list of what was included when your version of Nginx was built. In the list that appears, if you can find `--with-http_spdy_module`, then congratulations: You already have SPDY included.

Figure 15.2 demonstrates this command running from my terminal.

If you do not see `--with-http_spdy_module` in the list when you run the command, you need to either update your Nginx installation from your Linux repository or download and build Nginx with `--with-http_spdy_module` as part of your configuration parameters.

Having support for SPDY does not mean that it is already enabled. To make sure your server is using it, you need to open your Nginx configuration file. If you do not know where your configuration file is, you should first look at `/etc/nginx/sites-available/`. For Ubuntu, the configuration file is called `default`.

Inside the configuration, you should have a section for your server that takes care of "secure" or HTTPS settings. The following shows a truncated sample of a configuration file:

```
server {
    listen 443 ssl;

    ssl_certificate server.crt;
    ssl_certificate_key server.key;
    ...
}
```

Figure 15.2 To make it easier to find, I have highlighted the required `--with-http_spdy_module`.

Adding `spdy` to the second line enables SPDY. The following shows how the second line should appear with SPDY enabled:

```
listen 443 ssl spdy;
```

Cache

Using a cache is one of the fastest and easiest ways to improve server stability and asset delivery. Scores of sites out there do not currently take advantage of a cache and suffer from going viral, or just from an increased load as more users start to use their site.

A cache works by storing frequently used files in memory instead of reading the files from a hard disk. The cache also takes files that would normally be created from dynamic resources and creates a static copy of them that will update either only as needed or on a schedule.

By serving static assets rather than dynamic ones, you save on your first time to byte (server response time), on excessive hits on your database, and on your server needing to compile your dynamic markup (PHP, ASP, JSP, and so on) into HTML every time a page is requested.

You might not have even thought that your server was doing any work to serve your site, but it is actually doing a considerable amount of work to keep all those requests queued up and served. Site traffic, especially when condensed in a short period of time, has been known to completely drop websites.

> **Tip**
>
> Some websites either cannot be cached or contain specific data that must be dynamic and thus cannot be cached. This is one of the primary reasons eCommerce websites tend to go down during massive sale events such as Black Friday and Double Eleven. To overcome some of these issues, you might need to create a queue where users are redirected by a load balancer to a "waiting" server until your main server has room to process them, or by serving as much static content as possible and using Ajax methods to request dynamic data. Just be sure to always let users know what is happening, and try to give them an estimate instead of a spinning circle.

When working with Apache, you might find a couple caching modules useful. The first is `mod_file_cache`, and the second is `mod_cache`.

`mod_file_cache` is used to keep track of the most requested files and move them into memory so that they are easily accessible and can be served as fast as possible. This means that if you are constantly editing files, replacing the same image with a new one, building dynamic pages, or otherwise tweaking your code, your files will not cache and you will not see an improvement.

To get started with `mod_file_cache`, you need to specify what files should be cached to memory on startup. This is done in your server configuration file by listing files in a space-delimited format. The following is an example of using `MMapFile`.

```
MMapFile /var/www/index.html /var/www/images/logo.png /var/www/contact.html
```

Using `MMapFile` places the file into memory. Even if the file is updated on disk, the changes will not be picked up until server restart.

Another caching option is to use `CacheFile`. This is similar to `MMapFile`; the difference is that pointers indicate where the files are stored in memory instead of pointing to the files themselves. You can think of this as an indexing or mapping operation in which the system knows exactly where to get the files without keeping them in memory all the time. Files to be cached are referenced in a space-delimited fashion just as they are when using `MMapFile`. The following is an example of using `CacheFile`.

```
CacheFile /var/www/media/level5.mp3 /var/www/media/demo.mp4
```

When using `mod_file_cache`, that is all there is to it. You just need to remember that when you make a change, your server must be restarted to pick up the changes.

The `mod_cache` module also leverages the power of `mod_mem_cache` and `mod_disk_cache`, allowing you to better cache static, dynamic, and even proxied content.

To get started, you need to enable `mod_mem_cache` if you have not already done so. You can do this by typing the following into your terminal:

```
sudo a2enmod mem_cache
```

After the command completes, you must restart your Apache server to pick up the configuration change.

> ### Tip
> You can make changes to many of your Apache modules by changing their configuration files. These files are generally stored in the `/etc/apache2/mods-available/` folder. Use `vi`, `vim`, or `nano` to open, view, and edit these files. Just remember to restart your Apache server after making changes, or they will not be picked up and incorporated.

Enabling `mod_disk_cache` follows the same steps as enabling `mod_mem_cache`. The following shows the command needed to enable the module:

```
sudo a2enmod disk_cache
```

After enabling the module, remember to restart your Apache server to pick up the changes.

If you want to fine-tune your caching setup, consult the official documentation by visiting http://httpd.apache.org/docs/2.2/caching.html to learn more about enabling and using `mod_file_cache` and `mod_cache` on your Apache server.

PageSpeed

Another module you might want to consider using with your server is the PageSpeed module, by Google (https://developers.google.com/speed/pagespeed/module). This module is the Swiss Army knife of content delivery. Some of the features that it brings to the table are listed here:

- Combines and minifies multiple JavaScript file requests into one file depending on configuration
- Combines multiple CSS files into one minified file
- Can break down small scripts or site assets and replace them as an inline asset

- Provides image processing for removable metadata, specific image size, and format encoding
- Removes whitespace

Each of these features is essential to making sure that your site is delivered to the end user in the fastest way possible. As unbelievable as it might seem, even when doing as much preprocessing as it does to return a requested page, it really does serve the page back faster. This is because of the following:

- Serving 1 to 10 HTTP requests is always faster than serving 50 to 200.
- Compressed and optimized images are smaller than uncompressed images.
- Deferring "blocking" assets allows the user to see and interact with the page sooner.
- Optimizing asset delivery for "above the fold" content gives users something to use while the rest of the page is loaded in the background.

PageSpeed can be used with Apache and Nginx and through a provider such as Dreamhost, GoDaddy, or edgecast, or through the PageSpeed Service (https://developers.google.com/speed/pagespeed/service).

PageSpeed with Apache

Installing and using PageSpeed on your Apache server is remarkably similar to setting up SPDY with Apache. If you are using Debian or Ubuntu, you need to download the `.deb` file and run the following command from your terminal:

```
sudo dpkg -i mod-pagespeed-*.deb
sudo apt-get -f install
```

After you have finished installation, you need to restart your Apache server to pick up changes. Apache enables PageSpeed after installation, but you need to do a few minor tweaks to be fully up and running. Visit https://developers.google.com/speed/pagespeed/module/configuration for troubleshooting advice and for situations that might apply to your version of Apache.

PageSpeed with Nginx

Unfortunately, Nginx does not have a module or preconfigured plugin to work with PageSpeed. This means that you need to build Nginx with PageSpeed included. To get started on Ubuntu, open your terminal and run the following:

```
sudo apt-get install build-essential zlib1g-dev libpcre3 libpcre3-dev
```

This installs the necessary tools to build Nginx. Next, you need to download `ngx_pagespeed` by running the following from your terminal:

```
cd ~
wget https://github.com/pagespeed/ngx_pagespeed/archive/
➥release-1.7.30.4-beta.zip
unzip release-1.7.30.4-beta.zip
cd ngx_pagespeed-release-1.7.30.4-beta/
wget https://dl.google.com/dl/page-speed/psol/1.7.30.4.tar.gz
tar -xzvf 1.7.30.4.tar.gz # expands to psol/
```

Note that this uses version 1.7.30.4-beta. Although that is the current version as of this writing, check to make sure you are downloading the proper version. Next, you need to actually perform the build of Nginx:

```
cd ~
# check http://nginx.org/en/download.html for the latest version
wget http://nginx.org/download/nginx-1.4.4.tar.gz
tar -xvzf nginx-1.4.4.tar.gz
cd nginx-1.4.4/
./configure --add-module=$HOME/ngx_pagespeed-release-1.7.30.4-beta
make
sudo make install
```

When you are finished with the build, Nginx should be able to take advantage of PageSpeed. Unlike Apache, Nginx does not turn on PageSpeed by default. You will need to edit your configuration file and add the following to every `server` block of code to enable it:

```
pagespeed on;

# Needs to exist and be writable by nginx.
pagespeed FileCachePath /var/ngx_pagespeed_cache;

location ~ "^/pagespeed_static/" { }
location ~ "^/ngx_pagespeed_beacon$" { }
location /ngx_pagespeed_statistics { allow 127.0.0.1; deny all; }
location /ngx_pagespeed_global_statistics { allow 127.0.0.1; deny all; }
location /ngx_pagespeed_message { allow 127.0.0.1; deny all; }
location /pagespeed_console { allow 127.0.0.1; deny all; }
location /pagespeed_admin { allow 127.0.0.1; deny all; }

# Ensure requests for pagespeed optimized resources go to the pagespeed
➥handler
# and no extraneous headers get set.
location ~ "\.pagespeed\.([a-z]\.)?[a-z]{2}\.[^.]{10}\.[^.]+" {
  add_header "" "";
}
```

After you change your configuration, remember to restart your server to pick up the changes. For further instruction on making edits to your server configuration, visit https://developers.google.com/speed/pagespeed/module/configuration.

PageSpeed Service

If you are not using CentOS, Fedora, Debian, or Ubuntu and you still want the power and flexibility that PageSpeed offers, you can sign up for the PageSpeed service. This is currently a free service from Google that you can leverage to get all the benefits of PageSpeed without going through server configuration and management.

Before you sign up, remember that if you are already heavily optimizing your own code (removing whitespace, using gzip/deflate compression, detecting support for WebP images and swapping out your JPEG images for them, and combining and minifying your CSS and JavaScript) and using a caching system, PageSpeed might not give you the boost you are thinking you will get.

To test how much faster your site will be using the service, go to www.webpagetest.org/compare and enter your URL. After the test has run, you will be presented with a report that compares your site loading normally with your site with the PageSpeed service optimizing your images, files, and asset requests.

Google is offering this service for free but might decide to charge for it in the future. Also note that if you need to support SSL, you will be charged for bandwidth through a Google Apps for Business account.

Summary

In this chapter, you learned about various web servers that are currently available and popular for web development. You also learned that you can use several plugins or modules to help deliver content in a fast and optimized way to your users.

You investigated the importance of setting up a server cache and how this can be accomplished in Apache with a few modules.

You then explored the SPDY module and how it is used with HTTP to optimize requests for delivery. You also saw how it can be added to an existing Apache server and learned that it is included with most new Nginx installations.

Finally, you learned about PageSpeed as both a server addition and a service. You saw the benefits that it provides and how to get started configuring it with your system.

CHAPTER 16

HIGH PERFORMANCE WITH DEVELOPMENT TOOLS

Creating the perfect mobile experience does not start and end with the design. It takes more than a clean-cut, content-rich design that is delivered from optimized servers. You also need to perform application audits to make sure that your site is in peak performance. Depending on your server infrastructure, you might also need to consider build tools that will concatenate, minify, and compress your site assets. In this chapter, you learn about these tools and how to leverage them.

Development Tools

A wide variety of tools are available for web developers. Some of these tools are bundled as services that can be purchased or subscribed to, and some are built into the devices and browsers you are using right now.

This chapter shows you the development tools that come bundled inside Google Chrome, Mozilla Firefox, and Microsoft Internet Explorer.

I also show you some tools that you might be able to leverage as part of your development process to create optimized assets that will work on less-than-perfect servers to help you with your content and asset delivery.

Browser Developer Tools

In the last few years, in-browser development tools have steadily improved. Gone are the days of developing a custom debugging application to watch the internals of your JavaScript application. Now we have tools that can monitor the frames per second of your page rendering, the time it takes to download an asset, and even the time needed to debug your JavaScript in real time with breakpoints.

Most modern browsers have a development tool that is included or that can be downloaded. Some browsers have even given their developer tools nicknames, such as Opera Dragonfly. For this book, I show you the developer tools that are included in Chrome, Firefox, and Internet Explorer.

Chrome DevTools

Chrome ships with a built-in set of developer tools nicknamed DevTools. You can access this incredibly featured toolset by pressing either Ctrl+Shift+i in Windows or pressing Command+Option+i in OS X.

You can also access the tools through the Option menu, or by right-clicking an object and choosing Inspect Element. Figure 16.1 shows the Chrome browser with the DevTools window open and ready for use.

The DevTools window might look overwhelming at first, so take a minute to familiarize yourself with it. Along the top of the window are sections that can be activated (with a click, or tap if you have a touchscreen monitor). Table 16.1 lists these sections and summarizes what each does.

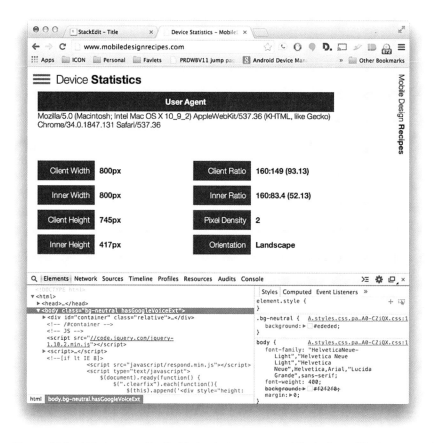

Figure 16.1   At first glance, the DevTools window appears at the bottom of the browser and looks like a mess of windows and code.

Table 16.1   Tool Sections of DevTools

Tool Section	Description
Elements	The left side of the screen shows the rendered DOM; you can manipulate data by double-clicking and then replacing current values with your own. The right side shows your applied, inherited, and computed styles. This enables you to also add custom styles and manipulate them on the fly.
Network	Every request that is passed from browser to server is visible here. This includes information on the protocol used, the request status code, the MIME type, and timings for the requested assets.
Sources	This section is used for looking at the files that the browser has downloaded, as well as setting up breakpoints and stepping through code as it renders.
Timeline	This section enables you to view how a page is rendered. You can use this section to view paint timings, see JavaScript rendering, and even track down how they overlap with each other.

Tool Section	Description
Profiles	In this section, you can observe the JavaScript CPU usage and your JavaScript memory allocation.
Resources	Here you can view parts of the browser that are generally hidden from users, such as session storage and local storage. Files that are loaded are also visible.
Audits	Running an audit on your site is like having instant access to PageSpeed Insights. Running an audit gives you information on how to improve your site load speed, the files you need to improve, and even how much of your CSS is used on the page you are viewing.
Console	The console displays everything from warnings and errors to messages through the `console.log()` function. To figure out where any JavaScript has broken, or even to run some JavaScript on the fly, the console is the section you will want to leverage.

When working with mobile devices and a mobile site, you will want to access another portion of DevTools. By pressing the Esc key on your keyboard or clicking an icon on the right side of the DevTools window, you can launch a special console drawer that contains a few extra options. Figure 16.2 shows which button to click, as well as what appears when activated.

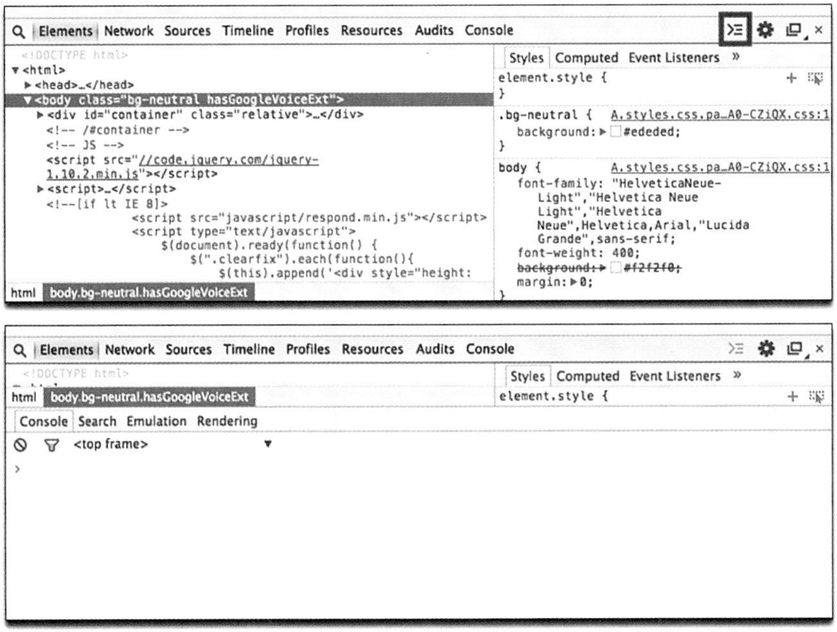

Figure 16.2 By activating the console drawer (top), you gain access to some very useful features (bottom).

Inside this drawer, you are given access to the console and also can access the Search, Emulation, and Rendering sections. Each of these sections offers you a robust solution.

The Emulation section is especially useful because of how it changes the way Chrome works. When you activate the Emulation section, you have a group of suboptions that enable you to emulate a particular device, change the screen size (including emulated pixel density), change the user agent that is sent from the browser, and emulate certain device features, such as geolocation coordinates and accelerometer data.

I encourage you to explore and become familiar with all these settings, but to quickly get your hands dirty, start with the Devices section and choose a device to emulate from the list. Figure 16.3 shows the list of devices that Chrome 34 can emulate.

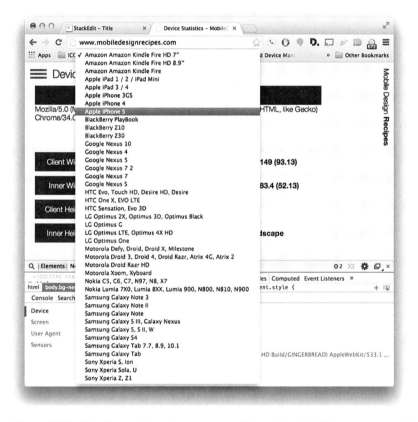

Figure 16.3   Selecting a device changes many of the settings that Chrome can emulate.

After selecting a device to emulate, you need only click the Emulate button to start emulating the device. As a precaution, I recommend refreshing the page you are on. When the page refreshes, you will view the page in the same manner as the device you are emulating. Figure 16.4 shows a page rendered in Chrome when emulating an iPhone 5.

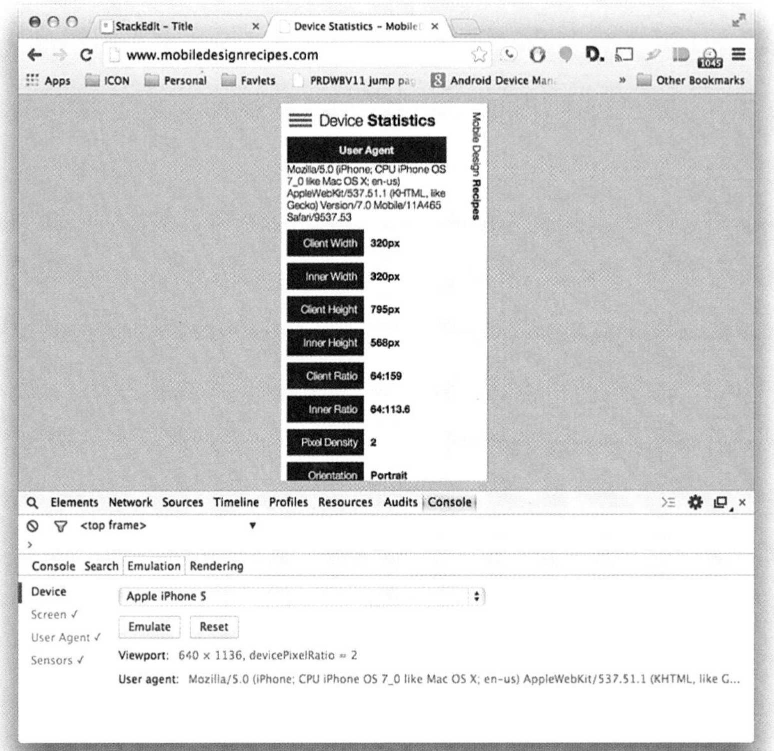

Figure 16.4 Not only has the screen been resized, but the user agent that the website detected matches an iPhone 5.

Emulating a mobile device is handy and can help you to "virtually" test your designs on the myriad devices you do not have. Note that emulation does not emulate the processor or video capabilities of a device. It does emulate the viewable area, the user agent, and the pixel density, which makes it a very powerful tool when creating responsive websites.

The last feature I cover for DevTools is a rather fantastic feature for debugging a website on the actual hardware viewing it.

> Tip
>
> To use Chrome and Android to do remote debugging, your computer and Android device must be running Chrome 32+. Your Android device must also have debugging mode enabled. In addition, you need to download the proper USB driver for your Android device. Check the manufacturer's website for the correct drivers. Visit https://developer.chrome.com/devtools/docs/remote-debugging for complete instructions on setting up remote debugging.

To get started, put your Android device into debugging mode and connect it to your computer using a USB cable. On your computer, click the menu button inside Chrome, and then choose Tools->Inspect Devices. A new tab appears, allowing you to check a box titled Discover USB Devices.

After checking the box, you are prompted on your Android device to accept an RSA fingerprint from your computer. Because you have created this connection, you can tap "OK" on your device to complete the connection.

When the connection completes, Chrome on your desktop lists the device and any open tabs that are available in Chrome for inspection. Clicking the Inspect link opens DevTools in a new window.

This window is connected to your device and allows you to do all the things you can do for your desktop browser. This includes inspecting the DOM, checking your network connections and timeline (which is useful when testing your mobile data connection), creating profiles, and running audits.

You can even perform a screencast of your mobile device to your desktop. This screencast is a two-way connection that enables you to control the mobile device from your desktop and also update the desktop on what you are doing from your device. Figure 16.5 shows the screencast enabled in DevTools.

Looking at Figure 16.5, you might have noticed that the top of the device screen appears to be transparent, or looks like a checkerboard. This is because of the "browser chrome" that is present on the mobile device. The browser chrome is the location bar, the tab control, and the menu button. This area hides when a user scrolls down and appears when a scroll-up is performed. Because I am at the top of the page, it is currently visible—and it explains why a "void" appears onscreen.

From here, you can inspect, change content, test, edit, and change styles (this is especially important for fonts and how they will render on a mobile device), as well as perform other functions.

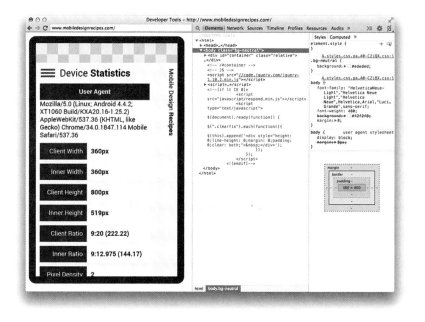

Figure 16.5   The device screen is broadcast to DevTools, enabling you to see close up how it is rendered.

I have only scratched the surface of everything DevTools is capable of. For more information on DevTools, visit the official site, at https://developers.google.com/chrome-developer-tools/.

Firefox

The Firefox browser has made some awesome progress in the last couple years in regard to not only the browser as a whole, but also development tools that give developers a leg up on creating better websites.

Using Firebug

The first tool that really made a difference for me as a developer using Firefox was the incredible Firebug plugin (https://www.getfirebug.com/). It allowed me to inspect the DOM and perform some analytical data of my site.

Today Firebug is still going strong and can be downloaded and installed into Firefox. After you have installed it, you can open it either by finding the little bug icon or by pressing the F12 key on your keyboard.

> **Tip**
>
> Firebug is known to cause some connection issues because it analyzes web traffic and browser performance. It is a fantastic tool to use while developing, but remember to close it when you are done developing and are ready to relax with some personal web surfing.

The Firebug window looks fairly close to the one displayed by Chrome DevTools. The order is changed a bit, and you'll find different options under the submenus. Figure 16.6 shows the Firebug window open in Firefox.

Figure 16.6 Familiar yet different, the Firebug window is ready to do some work.

Similar to DevTools, Firebug enables you to inspect the DOM, check the structure of CSS and JavaScript, and also see how long it takes to download assets and view any status codes about them as they complete (or fail to load).

You might wonder why you would even bother using another tool when you have already seen the DevTools that Chrome offers. The easiest explanation is also the simplest.

Browsers are different.

You can pick your favorite metaphor here, but I'm going to go with snowflakes. All snowflakes are made from frozen water, and no snowflake is exactly the same. This applies directly to browsers. Every browser runs a different rendering engine, the heart or core of the browser. It takes the HTML, CSS, and JavaScript that is sent to it and assembles it into the web page that you view. This is also why some browsers are "faster" than others and why some use more system memory than others. An error you see in Chrome might be driving you nuts, but until you try it in Firefox and get a similar yet slightly different error, you might not know how to solve it.

Coverage of this plugin is light because the Mozilla team has stepped up in a big way to the included native developer tools of Firefox. If you have specific questions about Firebug, visit the FAQ (https://getfirebug.com/faq/) to learn more.

Using Firefox Developer Tools

The built-in developer tools that Firefox now boasts are an impressive set. They come bundled with Firefox, so you only need to press Command+Option+I (OS X) or Ctrl+Shift+I (Windows) to open the Developer Tools window. You can also access them through the menu by clicking the menu icon, then clicking Developer, and finally clicking Toggle Tools to open or close the Developer Tools window.

You might be wondering what sets the Firefox developer tools apart from both Firebug and Chrome DevTools. In short, the following helps make the difference:

- Responsive Design Mode
- JavaScript Scratchpad
- 3D view (or tilt)

Responsive Design Mode is a simple solution that helps you quickly resize the browser to various device sizes. The shortcut or hotkey to enable this mode is Command+Option+M (OS X) or Ctrl+Shift+M (Windows). Figure 16.7 shows the mode enabled for a 320x480 screen.

Inside this view, you can take screenshots, emulate touch events, and change the emulated window size by using the control buttons at the top. You can also add your own presets by sizing the screen to the dimension you want and then using the drop-down menu to click Add Preset. After a preset has been added, you can remove it by first selecting that preset and then using the drop-down menu to select Remove Preset.

The Scratchpad is a handy little window that you can use for keeping notes and snippets and for interacting with JavaScript files on your system. You can open and save JavaScript files, and you can even use the built-in Pretty Print feature to spruce up your code a bit.

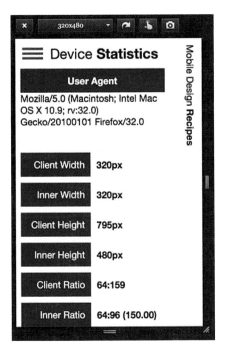

Figure 16.7 This view is not a fully accurate emulation of a mobile device screen, but it does allow you to mimic the resolution of a device.

You can run code directly from Scratchpad by typing it in and then clicking the Run button. You can give it a try to see how it works by doing a quick `alert()` message:

```
alert("This was generated from the Scratchpad!");
```

The other feature that sets the Firefox developer tools apart is the 3D view. This was a fun experiment at first, but it has developed into a developer tool staple (especially when dealing with multiple layers and off-canvas navigation).

When you click the 3D toggle button on the toolbar of Developer Tools, your window zooms out; you can then click and drag the screen to view your site rendered in 3D. Figure 16.8 shows a site rendered in 3D.

This is definitely not just a built-in parlor trick. This mode enables you to find specific elements, view their layering, and determine the type of element they are.

As Figure 16.8 demonstrates, the off-canvas elements of the page were clearly visible, allowing you to see what elements are rendered when the page is and what might be using some precious device memory.

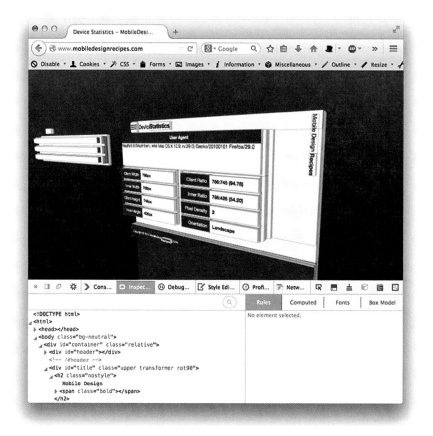

Figure 16.8   Notice that off-canvas elements are visible in 3D. This can help you find missing elements and elements that will load even if they are not "visible" on loading.

> **Tip**
>
> Using assets such as images for "loaders" might seem like a good idea, but that asset, even when loaded off-canvas, is still rendered and running on load. Depending on the file size or intensity of CPU usage, you might want to skip preloading your loaders and just invoke them as needed.

You can learn more about the Firefox Developer Tools, including how to install the Firefox OS Simulator, by visiting https://developer.mozilla.org/en-US/docs/Tools.

Internet Explorer

With the release of Internet Explorer (IE) 8 Microsoft bundled a rudimentary set of tools that developers could use to do some DOM inspection, logging, and debugging of JavaScript and JScript.

As with other developer tools, they shared a familiar layout, either attached or detached from the browser window and enabled you to switch between sections and submenus with a few button clicks.

The initial offering even enabled you to switch between the IE 6, 7, and 8 rendering modes. This was extremely useful because you could determine whether your "new for IE 8" design would work when rendered by users on IE 6.

Fast-forward to the present, and the tool set has changed for the better. A modern design that matches the theme in Windows 8 was added, along with new options to help you debug and develop. Figure 16.9 shows both the original IE 8 and the improvements made to the Developer Tools in IE 11.

Figure 16.9
Comparing the original (top) Developer Tools to the current ones (bottom), you can see that the theme, section placement, and even available options have changed.

With the new Developer Tools, you can do all the things that were available in the IE 8 version and much more. These sections are available in the latest version of IE Developer Tools:

- **DOM Inspector:** The DOM Inspector enables you to see the rendered DOM and to drill down through all the elements that make up your document. You can also toggle styles on and off, as well as add your own inline styles that will be applied until the page is reloaded. This means you can manipulate and try different styles before applying them to your actual stylesheet.

- **Console:** In the Console section, you can view errors, warnings, and logging information. You can filter the result set by toggling these different messages on and off. You can also run JavaScript from the Console window.

- **Debugger:** The Debugger is used on any JScript or JavaScript files you are using. You can open any file that is included in the site payload and add breakpoints that you can then step through to help you pinpoint any exceptions or data loss, or to check values.

- **Network:** In the Network section, you can record the assets that are downloaded, the time it takes to download them, and the status of each asset when it is requested. Unlike other Developer Tools, the tool works only when it is set to record network traffic. As a bonus, you can clear your cache and disable cookies to emulate what loading a page would look like to a new visitor with an empty cache.

- **UI Responsiveness:** The UI Responsiveness tool gives you a detailed look at how your page handles when it is being loaded, scrolled, or otherwise manipulated. Figure 16.10 shows a sample profile that was taken on a page with a slide nav. Knowing how your site renders, how it uses CPU, and the number of frames per second (FPS) it is running at goes a long way toward ensuring that your site works as efficiently and beautifully as possible.

- **Profiler:** The Profiler section traces the functions that are called and invoked on your page. This can help you track down excessive DOM manipulations, math calculations, and other redundant operations.

- **Memory:** The Memory tool profiles the memory usage of a tab over time. This can be a serious time saver when users are reporting crashes on a site but are not exactly sure where or why they happen. By profiling the memory usage during your session, you can see where memory is spiking and where the browser is being asked to perform more work. You can also take memory heap snapshots and use them for comparison. The heap snapshots include the number of objects in memory, which can help you determine whether you are doing too much work on the client.

- **Emulation:** Emulation enables you to change the "document mode," which is a set of rules used to render a web page. Note that Edge always loads the most current rendering set of rules. You can also change between desktop and Windows Phone rendering, as well as change the user agent that is reported to the server. The reported orientation, resolution, and geolocation values can also be set here to determine how a page will react based on available information.

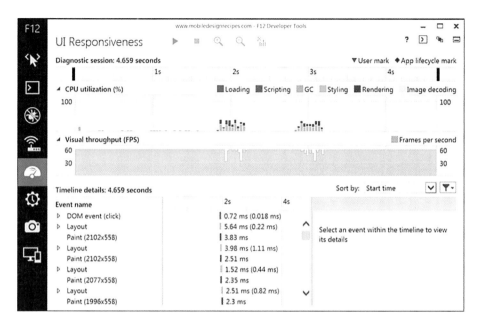

Figure 16.10 Note that the Visual throughput (FPS) section shows you that the frame rate drops when the slide menu is toggled on and off.

> **Tip**
>
> The rendering engine of IE 11 is massively different from the rendering engine used in IE 8. This means that even when "emulating" the IE 8 rendering engine in IE 11 using Developer Tools, you will not see the same things that IE 8 users see.

Because of the nature of web development, if you find that you still need to cater to a legacy version of IE, I strongly recommend that, instead of using Developer Tools to use an emulated browsing engine, you go to http://modern.ie/ and download a virtual machine. These virtual machines are free to use for 30-day periods and can be reinstalled when needed for development.

Build Tools

You have seen some of the browser developer tools that can help you debug and fine-tune your application, but you can use other tools as part of your development process as well. Using build tools can help you build faster prototypes, create optimized sites, and in a pinch, keep the plugins used in your sites up-to-date.

Grunt

Grunt (http://gruntjs.com/) is a task runner. It enables you to script or automate manual tasks that you would otherwise have to do. Another way to look at Grunt is that it is the cron for web development.

> ## Tip
>
> cron is a job scheduler for UNIX systems. These systems use a cron table, or crontab, to schedule various tasks that routinely need to be performed on a system. These tasks can be as simple as deleting files in a temporary directory or as complex as scripts that move, rename, sort, and even upload files from one place to another.

Grunt is an incredibly powerful tool because of the plugins that you can use with it. Plugins are available to minify or uglify code, compress images, combine file assets, compile Sass and LESS CSS files on saving, and even live-reload your browser.

Getting started with Grunt is fairly easy. First, you need to make sure that you have NodeJS installed (http://nodejs.org/). When you have NodeJS up and running, you can use `npm` to install Grunt. The following shows how to install Grunt globally:

```
npm install -g grunt-cli
```

> ## Tip
>
> Installing an app "globally" in regard to NodeJS means that you can execute the script from the command line anywhere. If you do not install an app or tool globally, you will be able to run that app only within the folder or project you installed it to. Keep in mind that not every package or app should be installed globally— just the ones you plan to use in multiple projects or most of the time.

After you install Grunt, you can create a file named `package.json` and another file named `Gruntfile.js`.

`package.json` should be familiar to NodeJS users. This file stores information about Grunt and any plugins or modules it will be using. The following is a sample `package.json` file:

```
{
  "name": "imagecomp",
  "version": "0.1.0",
  "devDependencies": {
    "grunt": "~0.4.1",
```

```
    "grunt-contrib-imagemin": "~0.4.0"
  }
}
```

`Gruntfile.js` is the file you will be using to configure the tasks that you would like Grunt to perform. The following is a rough skeleton that you can use as a starting point for Grunt:

```
module.exports = function(grunt) {
  grunt.initConfig({
    pkg: grunt.file.readJSON('package.json'),
    // plugin specifics go here
    plugin: {
      // config for plugin goes here
    }
  });
  grunt.loadNpmTasks('grunt-contrib-plugin');
  grunt.registerTask('default', ['plugin']);
};
```

In the previous code, you can see that I have used the term `plugin` in multiple places. This symbolizes various plugins you might be using. For example, if you were using the `imagemin` plugin, you would replace `plugin` with `imagemin` in the previous code. However, make sure that you have read the documentation for the plugin you are trying to use. For example, the `imagemin` plugin requires some further configuration to execute properly.

After you have configured your file and listed your dependencies in your `package.json` file, you can execute your Grunt setup by typing `grunt` from the terminal.

For a complete list of plugins, visit http://gruntjs.com/plugins. For a more comprehensive guide for getting started, visit http://gruntjs.com/getting-started.

Gulp

Another task runner that you might want to consider is Gulp (http://gulpjs.com/). It is really similar to Grunt: You can use various plugins, configure tasks, and run it from the command line. Gulp also requires NodeJS to be installed on your machine to use it.

Installing Gulp is almost the same as installing Grunt. From a terminal window, type the following:

```
npm install -g gulp
```

You should also run the following to save Gulp to your project dependencies:

```
npm install --save-dev gulp
```

Unlink Grunt, Gulp does not require a `package.json` file to run. Instead, you only need to create a file named `gulpfile.js` that will be used for processing.

The following is a sample setup of `gulpfile.js` used to compress images:

```
var gulp = require('gulp');
var gutil = require('gulp-util');
var imagemin = require('gulp-imagemin');

gulp.task('default', function(){
  gulp.src('images/**/*')
    .pipe(imagemin({ progressive: true, interlaced: true }))
    .pipe(gulp.dest('imagescomp'));
});
```

Gulp handles tasks by streaming them together when it processes, so in the previous example, you can see that three variables are defined: `gulp`, `gutil`, and `imagemin`. These are used in a chainlike or streaming fashion. First, `gulp` has the function `task()` run on it where it sets a value for an image path, and then it sends that data to the `imagemin` variable through the `pipe()` method. This sets some options and then passes the data back to `gulp` to allow it to set where the files should be placed after `imagemin` has processed them.

This type of processing data offers you a quick setup without requiring you to manage multiple files. For some people, this might also make more sense than building configurations and then registering and calling them as tasks.

If you are interested in using Gulp but already have a favorite Grunt plugin, you might be happy to know that many plugins have been ported to Gulp. For a list of plugins that you can use with Gulp, visit http://gulpjs.com/plugins/.

Summary

In this chapter, you learned about the developer tools that can help make debugging and creating sites easier.

You learned about the built-in developer tools that come with Chrome, Firefox, and Internet Explorer. These tools share similarities but also have several unique strengths that were highlighted as tools for you to leverage. You even learned that virtual machines can be used so that Linux and OS X developers can still test their work in IE.

You then explored the Grunt and Gulp build tools that are available for setting up and running your projects during the development phase. You examined some sample configuration files and saw a high-level view of what these files contain. Finally, you got some links to learn more and start using them.

INDEX

Numerics

960 Grid System, 31

A

A List Apart, 56, 119
accordions, 104
adaptive grids, 34-36
    advantages of, 36
    combining with responsive grids, 37
    disadvantages of, 36
adaptive layout, 100-101
adding modal windows, 107
address lists, 40
adjusting box model rendering with CSS, 58
Adobe Typekit, 92
advantages
    of adaptive grids, 36
    of implementing device database, 191
    of JavaScript device detection, 188
    of reading the UA string, 190
    of responsive grids, 34
Akamai, 132
alert() function, 166
anchor elements, adding Click to Call
  button, 106
Android
    design guides, 12
    fragments, 158
    screen resolutions, 16
    user expectations, 12
Android Metrics and Grids, 106
Apache web servers, 198, 207
APIs, DOM, 176-180
    Shadow DOM, 177-178
Apple Retina screens, 18
applications, 41
arranging content in columns, 104
artifacting, 143

aspect ratio, 137
assigning viewport measurements, 64
asynchronous delivery, 10
audio element, 172-173
autocapitalization, disabling, 109
autocorrection, disabling, 109

B

Bing Webmaster tools, 12
block-level layout, 96-98
    fold, handling, 98
Bootstrap, 29
bounce rate, 152
breakpoints, 72-78
    for navigation components, 102
Brick, 182-183
Brightcove, 132-133
browsers
    asynchronous delivery, 10
    development tools
        Chrome DevTools, 212-218
        Firefox developer tools, 218-222
        IE Developer Tools, 223-225
    IE8, scaling images, 118
    measurement values support, 66
    media query support, 72-73
    picture element support, 124
    rem units, support for, 62
build tools
    Grunt, 226-227
    Gulp, 227-228
building multiple tables, 49-51
buttons
    Click to Call, 106-107
    download button, building, 51-53
    menu buttons, 22
BXSlider, 105

C

X-Y-Z